THE SENATE SPECIAL REPORT ON Y2K

THE SENATE
SPECIAL REPORT
ON Y2K

Senator Robert F. Bennett, Chairman

Senator Christopher J. Dodd, Vice Chairman

THOMAS NELSON PUBLISHERS®
Nashville

Foreword by Gary North copyright © 1999 by Thomas Nelson, Inc.

Published in Nashville, Tennessee, by Thomas Nelson, Inc.

The Bible version used in this publication is the KING JAMES
VERSION of the Holy Bible.

Book design by Mark McGarry

ISBN 0-7852-6851-0

Printed in the United States of America.
1 2 3 4 5 6 — 04 03 02 01 00 99

THE SENATE SPECIAL REPORT ON Y2K

I close with this observation about the importance of this entire issue. One of the experts with whom I have been in contact since I assumed this new chairmanship said to me, "The one thing we know for sure about this is that nobody has ever done it before. We have no historical precedent to guide us, to tell us how to handle this and what we can expect." And, of course, he was accurate. Of course, that is a true summation of where we are.

Yet when I made that comment to another friend of mine, he said something that I think summarizes exactly the challenge we are facing. He said, "No, Bob, that is not true. We have a historic example." I said, "What is it?" He said, "the Tower of Babel."

He said, "The people got together and decided they were going to build a tower to heaven, and God didn't like it, so he fixed it so they could not talk to each other and that ended it." He said, "That is the paradigm of what we are dealing with here, Y2K." We are facing the possibility that after January 1 [2000] we cannot talk to each other because the world is all wired by computers, and if, indeed, that turns out to be the case, as was the case in Genesis, that will end it.

Senator Robert Bennett
Congressional Record (May 11, 1998)

Foreword

Gary North

www.garynorth.com

And the whole earth was of one language, and of one speech. And it came to pass, as they journeyed from the east, that they found a plain in the land of Shinar; and they dwelt there. And they said one to another, Go to, let us make brick, and burn them thoroughly. And they had brick for stone, and slime had they for morter. And they said, Go to, let us build us a city and a tower, whose top may reach unto heaven; and let us make us a name, lest we be scattered abroad upon the face of the whole earth. And the LORD came down to see the city and the tower, which the children of men builded. And the LORD said, Behold, the people is one, and they have all one language; and this they begin to do: and now nothing will be restrained from them, which they have imagined to do. Go to, let us go down, and there confound their language, that they may not understand one another's speech. So the LORD scattered them abroad from thence upon the face of all the earth: and they left off to build the city. Therefore is the name of it called Babel; because the LORD did there confound the language of all the earth: and from thence did the LORD scatter them abroad upon the face of all the earth. (Genesis 11:1–9)

In a civilization long, long ago, in a region far, far away, men shared the same language. More than this: they shared the same dream. Their dream was this: achieving autonomy from God. They chose to make a name for themselves. That is, they sought to define themselves and their world apart from God. They began to build a tower that would testify to their dreams, efforts, and skills down through ages to come. Their tower would link heaven and earth, stretching upward to heaven from the earth. Man would define the creation and put God in His place.

And God said, "I don't think so."

Men in those days feared being scattered. God scattered them. They dreamed of perpetual unity. God divided them. They confessed with one tongue the glories of man and the works of man's hand. God broke apart this humanistic collective by giving mankind a multitude of tongues. What seemed to be a simple cause—multiple languages—had permanent, comprehensive consequences. The society of Babel disappeared. Such is the fate of every New World Order that challenges the kingdom of God (Daniel 2:44).

It now appears that we are going to get another opportunity to experience at least part of this social cause-and-effect relationship in action. Let us pray that we do not have to experience all of it.

Digital Idiot Savants

In the movie *Rainman,* the Dustin Hoffman character remembered everything. And could he count! A spilled box of matches (minus four). Cards in a Las Vegas casino. He could work mental miracles. But he was stubborn and barely controllable. He had to be institutionalized. He was an idiot savant.

Today, the inmates are in charge of the asylum: computers. We have delegated to computers the operation of our complex life-support systems, which include what mainframe computer programmer Steve Heller has called society's *iron triangle:* electricity, telecommunications, and banking. To this list add agriculture, water/sewers, energy, medical services, capital markets, transportation, national defense, and everything produced by the companies on the Standard & Poor's 500.

Then add the output of the rest of the industrial world, including (especially) Asia. (When you think of economic repercussions, think "noncompliant Japanese banks.")

During the last thirty-five years—ever since the introduction of the IBM 360 computer in 1964—we have expanded output and cut costs through a worldwide delegation of data-management operations. We have become an information society. Meanwhile, we have slashed manufacturing and marketing expenses by an ingenious system called *just-in-time production.* Most businesses no longer carry large inventories. The information savings that computers have provided have enabled managers to create complex systems of production—systems so complex that only computers can run them. Workers create products on assembly lines supplied by 18-wheelers or UPS trucks that pulled up to the door early this morning. Today, those trucks are the mobile warehouses that sustain the nation's economy. More than this: *they sustain our entire society.* The week that those trucks stop rolling is the week that the world's economy begins to disintegrate.

Four words can cause this disintegration: "Our computer is down." Every time someone utters these four words, someone else's plans will be disrupted: depositor, worker, employer, patient, soldier, banker, tax collector. This is the heart of the matter: *the unexpected, computer-enforced revision of billions of plans.* We cannot revise our plans at zero cost, or anything close to zero cost, given the magnitude of the problem.

When mainframe programmers adopted the space-saving technique of dropping the 1 and the 9 in the century date, and then programming computers to insert these two digits automatically, they created the conditions for a worldwide crisis. When computers read oo as 1900 instead of 2000, and begin making calculations by adding or subtracting from 1900 instead of 2000, the phrase, "Our computer is down," will become widespread, all over the world, and all at the same time. Well, close to the same time. This phrase is beginning to be heard now. It will escalate as 2000 approaches. It will continue for the first few months in 2000. The question is: In the summer of 2000, what will remain of the worldwide social order that relied on computers?

A Systemic Problem

When noncompliant computers stay on, but operate in terms of inaccurate calculations, then the complex systems that they control will begin to behave erratically. That will be worse than a shutdown, which at least warns managers that they have a major problem. Bankruptcies will increase. So will unemployment.

It gets worse. The bad calculations made by computer A will be passed on—into computers B, C, and D, and from them to computers E, F, and G. This will be done through high-speed telephone lines, assuming that the telephone systems stay up. (They, too, are controlled by computers, including microchips with programs burned into them.)

The Year 2000 bug acts as a virus. It spreads from noncompliant computers to compliant ones, corrupting the digital information in the compliant ones. This means that programmers who are repairing the noncompliant programs must somehow devise digital filters that keep out inaccurate data coming in from noncompliant computers. How? How can all-purpose logical filters be designed to recognize inaccurate calculations and keep them out of compliant computers? There is almost no public discussion of this problem because there is no agreed-upon programming solution. That for which there is no universal solution is deliberately ignored.

Then there is the question of systems. Consider banking. Say that a large multinational bank is made Y2K-compliant.[1] As of mid-March 1999, no such bank exists anywhere on earth. Not one. Not after four years of work and billions of dollars of programming expenses. But, for the sake of argument, assume that a few of them do meet the January 1 deadline. How can they continue to operate if their digital filters reject data from thousands of noncompliant banks? What happens to the banking *system* when compliant banks dare not accept digital data from noncompliant banks? There is no operational answer for this problem, or at least none that has been discussed publicly. We are facing the breakdown of the banking system and every other computerized industry.

This is why I have been saying since 1996 that *Y2K is a systemic problem*. It is everywhere. It must be fixed simultaneously by all participants in a production system if the system is to survive. It is not good enough to make company A compliant if companies B, C, and D are noncompliant. It is an all-or-nothing problem within every industry.

General Motors' Y2K programmers have two billion lines of code to go through in search of century date errors.[2] If and when they finish correcting this code, testing the repaired code, repairing the glitches they inserted when correcting the code, testing again, and correcting again, General Motors will still face a supply lines problem. It has 100,000 suppliers.[3] What if any of these suppliers do not fix their computers? Then GM must find ways to communicate with them other than by computer. What if some of them go out of business? Then GM must find replacement suppliers—in months or weeks or days. What if GM cannot locate replacement suppliers? Ford, Chrysler, Honda, and the other auto manufacturers face the same problem. If key suppliers go bankrupt, auto companies must shut down their assembly lines.

Then what happens to GM's 100,000 suppliers? To their banks? To their employees?

In the summer of 1998, about 10,000 GM workers went on strike. Within a month, 200,000 GM workers were on unpaid temporary leave. The assembly lines had ceased to roll. GM settled with the strikers. The problem is, you cannot settle with a noncompliant computer. It is as uncooperative as an idiot savant whose routine has been disrupted. It does not care that you are being inconvenienced. It does not listen to reason. It does what it was programmed to do, or else it shuts down. And when it shuts down, it takes with it some of your plans and some of mine.

If enough of them shut down, we will all have to revise our plans—fast.

Think through one day's activities. What if, every time you tried to complete a transaction or use a service run by a computer, you received this message? "Our computer is down." Or what if you received no message at all? You just could not get the service. Begin with electricity. You flip the switch. Nothing happens. You go to the phone. No dial tone. And so on, through the day.

If you want a good introduction to this problem, go to the library and rent a copy of the first installment of James Burke's 1979 TV series, *Connections*. (If you cannot locate the video, read Chapter 1 of his book.) The first show is titled "The Trigger Effect." It deals with what happened on November 9, 1965, beginning at 5:15 P.M., when the power grid failed in the northeastern United States, including New York City. Burke then extends this scenario to what would happen if electrical power shut down everywhere. Where would you go? What would you do? How would you survive?[4]

You think, *This cannot happen.* You are wrong. It can happen. The power industry's experts say it can happen. They all add that it probably will not happen, but it can happen. You must now decide: Will this happen? Why won't it happen? And after you decide, you had better act consistently with what you have concluded.

The question of the power grid leads us to the February 24, 1999, Report of the Senate's Special Committee on the Year 2000 Technology Problem. It says, "There are no comprehensive studies concerning the number of entities that would have to fail to put the entire grid at risk, but some experts suggest that it may be a very small percentage if in key locations" (p. 36). It says a lot more. As you read it, keep thinking of the lyric of the old spiritual, *Dry Bones:* "The knee bone's connected to the thigh bone." Connections. The Y2K problem is all about connections. Broken connections.

A Very Special Committee

The U.S. Senate's Special Committee on the Year 2000 Technology Problem really is special. It is bipartisan. I know of no other committee in Congress that can plausibly make this claim. Alone among congressional committees, it has a chairman and a vice-chairman from rival political parties. On all other congressional committees, the minority party's senior member is called the "ranking member," not vice-chairman.

There is a reason for this bipartisanship. The Year 2000 Millennium Bug is a true bipartisan threat. Think of it as an equal opportunity destroyer.

The Special Committee came into existence on April 2, 1998. Since that time, the committee has held a series of hearings on these topics: utilities, healthcare services, telecommunications, transportation, financial services, general government services, general business, litigation, food supply, and the food industry.[5] On February 24, 1999, the committee published a report summarizing its findings, *Investigating the Impact of the Year 2000 Problem.* It was released to the public on Tuesday, March 2. This is the report you have in your hand.

The report is really, truly frightening. Strip out all of the qualifying language (hopeful but unsubstantiated opinion), and you have a series of problems listed for which there are no proven answers. There are hopes, but no answers. There are calming words and no Y2K-compliant, tested organizations.

In contrast to this report were the prepublication media efforts by Senators Bennett and Dodd to calm the public. It is important to understand that the two of them put a special spin on the Special Committee's report. On Sunday, February 28, they appeared on Sunday TV talk shows. Bennett appeared on *Face the Nation*. Dodd appeared on *Meet the Press*. These shows are part of what used to be called the Sunday Afternoon Intellectual Ghetto. They are aimed at people who are interested in current events, especially politics. The fact that a Senate committee could send senators of rival political parties to spread the same message is highly significant. What was the message? Here is how it was described by a March 1 Reuters news service story that was posted on Excite, a World Wide Web news site.

> Americans should prepare for the year 2000 computer bug like they would a hurricane, by stocking up on canned food and bottled water in case vital services are cut off, senators leading a congressional study of the problem said Sunday.
>
> Global trade could also be disrupted because major U.S. trading partners, including Japan and oil producers Venezuela and Saudi Arabia, may not be able to address the computer glitch in time, Utah Republican Sen. Robert Bennett and Connecticut Democratic Sen. Christopher Dodd said.
>
> "This problem is real," Bennett, chairman of the Senate's special committee on the so-called Y2K problem, told CBS's "Face the Nation." "This will not be the end of the world as we know it. But we have to stay on top of it." . . .
>
> Bennett and Dodd, who is vice chairman of the Senate's Y2K committee, are expected to release their report on the computer problem Tuesday.
>
> According to a draft copy of the report, the nation's airports started preparations too late, and shipments of goods and services by sea could be disrupted because the maritime industry was running behind.
>
> "It's not unwise for people to do a little stockpiling," Dodd told NBC's "Meet the Press."
>
> He said people should buy bottled water, canned goods and other essentials as they might to prepare for a "good storm, a hurricane" that would last two to three days.
>
> Dodd said people should also keep copies of their financial

records in case banks run into unforeseen problems. But he said that banking problems were unlikely.

There was no need for people to buy electricity generators or stockpile propane because a prolonged nationwide blackout was unlikely, Bennett said.

The committee's draft report added that due to limited resources and a lack of awareness, rural and inner-city hospitals across the United States would be at high risk. It said more than 90 percent of doctors' offices had yet to address the problem.

The draft report concluded that more serious problems could strike other countries, including some major U.S. trading partners far behind in Y2K readiness . . .

Japan and Mexico were also at serious risk, along with France, Germany, Brazil, Italy and Spain, according to the report . . .

But both senators said there was no way to tell how serious the disruptions would be.

"When we get to New Year's Eve, everybody, no matter how informed we think we are, is going to be holding his breath," Bennett said.

Notice the focus of this bipartisan message: the big problems will be mostly foreign. The United States will have some problems, but not big ones. Foreigners, however, should experience far worse problems. My assessment: if we see Japan, Saudi Arabia, France, and Germany go into an economic depression, we will learn to what extent the knee bone's connected to the thigh bone, economically speaking.

The term *hurricane* has been used repeatedly by those few organizations and individuals who have warned about Y2K. A hurricane lasts for a few hours. Then the sun comes out again. The problem is, we know from experience that people in the path of a hurricane refuse to stock up until twenty-four hours or less before the weatherman says it will hit.

Another phrase, "seventy-two hours," has also become popular to describe the time horizon of Y2K-based disruptions. Somehow, the computer code that has resisted correction by teams of programmers ever since 1995 will be fixed in three days over the New Year holidays, in the middle of a worldwide crisis. This is exactly what the public wants to hear.

This spin was remarkably successful. In the month of March, the public's interest in Year 2000 seminars began fading. Gold coin sales by the U.S. Mint fell off. In February, the Mint had announced that it had reached its production limits and would begin rationing American eagle gold coins to wholesalers. The psychology of many Y2K-alarmed people—a tiny minority of the U.S. population—turned around overnight, despite the fact that the computer code was still broken, and noncompliant organizations, their employees, and their customers were just as vulnerable as they had been in February.

Senator Bennett has repeatedly compared himself to Paul Revere. He has proclaimed this model on the Committee's Web site. "We must be Paul Revere. We must tell everyone that Y2K is coming. But we must not be Chicken Little and tell them that the sky is falling." But by March 1999, his message had changed. He had toned down his warning. He was obviously afraid of becoming Chicken Little. It was as if Paul Revere had ridden across the Massachusetts countryside, shouting to all who would listen, "The British are coming, the British are coming, but they're carrying only peashooters." Everyone would have rolled over and gone back to sleep.

You must decide: Will it be economic peashooters, muskets, machine guns, or nuclear weapons? And after you decide, your checkbook stubs had better start reflecting your assessment.

Read the actual report, which so few reporters did before writing up their summaries of Bennett's remarks to the media. The report does not focus on foreigners, nor did the hearings on which it is based. It deals with the United States. What it says is that there could be extensive problems in the United States in 2000. This is not what the politicians are saying.

Senator Bennett on the Fate of a Civilization

The constant refrain of the politicians is that no one knows what will happen. This message is supposed to calm voters, which it usually does. But this element of uncertainty ought to be interpreted in the light of what the report reveals. What it reveals is this: in each of the areas surveyed, there is not one Y2K-compliant company or organization. "We're working on it," the representatives testified. But not one of them announced that his organization was compliant.

Here is a syllogism worthy of Aristotle, Aquinas, and even Casey Stengel: "If no organization in an industry is Y2K-compliant, then the industry is not Y2K-compliant." This sounds absurdly obvious—a truism, even a platitude. But the survival of Western civilization hangs on it. If the worldwide division of labor that has given us our wealth—goods and services that have sustained life for six billion people—collapses in 2000 because the digital idiot savants no longer communicate accurately with one another, then we will experience a catastrophe on a scale undreamed of as recently as 1995.

On July 14, 1998, President Clinton and Vice President Gore delivered a pair of luncheon speeches on Y2K to the National Academy of Sciences. These speeches received no attention by the media, nor were they intended to. Had the president wanted publicity on this topic, he would have held a press conference or spoken at the annual convention of some powerful voting bloc. The next day, Senator Bennett spoke to the National Press Club in Washington, D.C. He praised the president for having said something on Y2K. He did not add, "better something than nothing." Then he delivered a rousing speech on Y2K. He made this controversial assessment:

> I believe we're going to win; that is I think that civilization as we know it is not going to come to an end. It's a possibility. Possibility, if Y2K were this weekend instead of seventy-six weekends from now, it would. But we have seventy-six weeks in which to

try to get this under control. But we are, in a sense, at war against this problem. And you would not have said in the Second World War, "Oh, because the president assures us we're going to eventually prevail, we do not need to cover Guadalcanal, Iwo Jima, Normandy, the Battle of the Bulge, or any of the rest of it."

Only rarely do we see any national politician make a statement like this in public, except during wartime. He then made a series of observations about the computer revolution:

And just as the concept of interchangeable parts transformed the world in the Industrial Revolution, the concept of digital code transformed the world in the Information Revolution. And we are living through that revolution in ways that future historians will look back on and comment about. But it has happened to us gradually enough that we don't really understand the incredible impact of that little notion that a switch can be either on or off, that a punch in an IBM card can either be in or out, or that a pit on a laser disk can be burned to either be there or not, only a micron wide so that on a disk this size, you can put the entire Encyclopedia Britannica and read it by virtue of digital code.

Enormously significant things have happened as a result of that revolution. We have now eliminated whole portions of the hierarchy of corporate organizations. Middle management is pretty well gone. Where did it go? It was replaced by computer technology, because the purpose of middle management was to manage information. Now, an individual on the factory floor can call up on a screen more information than he could have gotten from acres and acres of Harvard MBAs in the middle management prior to the invention of the computer and digital code.

And it has become ubiquitous this digital code. It is everywhere we look. One of the things that has happened—and I am going to focus on this for just a minute out of my business background, to help you understand how difficult the Y2K challenge is—is that we have changed manufacturing fundamentally, and not just by robotics and all of the things you think of in terms of computers.

Go back twenty-five years ago to General Motors, and they would have warehouses filled with steel and aluminum and glass and rubber and chrome and all the other things necessary to produce a car. And usually there would be about ninety days—(audio break). (Following audio break)—in these warehouses.

Along came digital code. Toyota pioneered Edward Deming's idea of "just in time" inventory. The warehouse holding the spare parts or the component parts of a Toyota consisted of the railroad car in which those parts arrived at the plant. And the railroad car pulls up to the side of the plant, they open the doors and start off-loading the parts directly onto the assembly line until the car is empty, and it is then pulled away and another car pulled up. You can imagine the savings—money, time, effort, capital, everything else—that has occurred because of "just in time" inventory. But you must understand that "just in time" inventory cannot work without computers. You cannot have enough middle managers with Harvard MBAs figuring it out to make it work if you don't have computers.

His comments were all true, and all terrifying. Here is why they were terrifying: his comments in the question-and-answer session that followed.

MR. HARBRECHT: Sir, a final question today from a veteran journalist. Why don't we just forget about all this computer nonsense and go back to using typewriters? Life was simpler in the old days. Your comment, please?

SEN. BENNETT: Well, first you're going to have to find one! (Laughter.)

But I go back to my statement when I gave you that somewhat convoluted description of how the economy has changed in the information age, we can't go back to typewriters. We can't go back to twenty-five years ago. We can't just forget about this problem because twenty-five years ago doesn't exist.

Somebody asked it in a different context, but the same question: "Why are we worried about the fact that the switches

that control the rail traffic in this country are all computerized? Let's go back to somebody standing there and throwing
the switch in advance of the train." There are no switches to
throw. All of the manual switches have been replaced.

You go back to your typewriter—the old city room is gone,
it's all computerized now, and the old Linotype machine is
gone. And what's on your screen in the city room is connected
to the typesetting computerized system, and you can't bring
the Linotype machine back; it only exists in a museum some-
where, and there are not enough museums to handle all the
newspapers that would need them, if we were to go back to
those days.

We cannot go back because the infrastructure that under-
girded our entire society twenty-five years ago has been dis-
mantled. It is gone. The skills are gone, the people are gone,
the equipment is gone. Like it or not, we have no choice in this
situation but to plow forward and, one way or the other, make
it work.

Conclusion

He was wrong. Of course we can go back. We just cannot go
back at zero price. The computers have been inadvertently programmed to push us back. To avoid this unwanted reversal, programmers must reprogram the computers and the digital data
inside them. But there is not enough time remaining to accomplish this. The Senate report is clear on this. The programmers
can repair only parts of the systems. Which parts? With what
effects? "The question is not will there be disruptions, but how
severe the disruptions will be" (p. 18). That is indeed the question. But the report is noncommittal: ". . . the fundamental
questions of risk and personal preparedness cannot be
answered at this time" (p. 2). Well, then, exactly when? We know
the answer. In 2001. Maybe.

Read this report. Read it very carefully. Your life may depend
on it, and your retirement plans surely do. Look for solid, verifiable evidence that proves that Senator Bennett's warning on

July 15, 1998, is not still valid. I find no such compelling evidence in this report. What I find is a series of hopeful statements from representatives of noncompliant companies that their industries will be compliant on January 1, 2000. I find strangely precise statements about being 76 percent compliant or 98 percent compliant. But if no companies within these industries are yet compliant and fully tested—and not one of them claims this status—then managers cannot know if their firm is 76 percent compliant or not. There is no successful example so far of a firm brought fully to tested compliance.

We live in a world economy. The international division of labor sustains us. This division of labor rests on international telecommunications and computerized data. It rests on banking, which is date-sensitive. It rests on the computerized electrical power grid. *We have turned over data management to idiot savants that have been programmed wrong.*

What next? Read the entire report. Then decide, not based on all the hopeful statements, but on the verifiable facts reported. Bear in mind also that the facts were reported by companies that were not under oath and were not checked out by independent third parties. As the report says, "Self-reporting has yielded unreliable assessments for most industry sectors. With few exceptions, disclosure of Y2K compliance is poor."

And as you read it, please remember: "The knee bone's connected to the thigh bone."

S. Prt. 106-10

**The United States Senate
Special Committee on the Year 2000 Technology Problem**

Senator Robert F. Bennett, Chairman
Senator Christopher J. Dodd, Vice Chairman

Investigating the Impact of the Year 2000 Problem

*Competing pressures tempt one to believe
that an issue deferred is a problem avoided:
more often it is a crisis invited.*

Henry Kissinger

**Summary of the Committee's
Work in the 105th Congress**

February 24, 1999

Robert F. Bennett, Utah, Chairman

Jon Eyl, Arizona
Gordon Smith, Oregon
Susan M. Collins, Maine
Ted Stevens, Alaska, *Ex Officio*

Christopher J. Dodd, Connecticut
Jeff Bingaman, New Mexico
Daniel Patrick Moynihan, New York
Robert C. Byrd, West Virginia, *Ex Officio*

United States Senate

SPECIAL COMMITTEE ON THE YEAR 2000
TECHNOLOGY PROBLEM
WASHINGTON, DC 20510-6486

February 24, 1999

Dear Colleagues:

The Special Committee on the Year 2000 Technology Problem was created on April 2, 1998, by unanimous consent of the Senate. Despite its short tenure, the Committee has logged a staggering number of hours addressing the Y2K issue, conducting interviews and writing letters to federal agencies, industry trade groups, and corporate executives. The Committee has conducted 10 hearings, asked difficult questions, and requested reports on a breathtaking range of affected industries. The Committee is among the most broad-based, best-informed bodies in existence, yet it cannot predict what will occur on January 1, 2000. The data simply does not exist.

The attached report embodies the Committee's best evaluation of the current Y2K environment. We have made a difference. By placing Y2K in the public eye, and by holding individuals publicly accountable for Y2K preparation, the Committee has engaged people and associations in the Y2K issue who otherwise may have remained ignorant of the significance of the Y2K problem.

We are pleased with the advances in awareness and Y2K remediation that we have seen since the inception of the Committee, but much work remains. In 1999, the Committee will continue to assess and hold hearings on the domestic sectors. While the Committee is growing more comfortable with the level of domestic preparedness, we have far less confidence in the international arena. For that reason, the level of international Y2K preparedness and the effects that poorly prepared countries may have on the United States will be a major focus of the Committee's work in the 106th Congress.

The Y2K problem is undoubtedly one of the most important issues we will face this year, and as such, deserves our top priority. I encourage each of you to read this report and engage the Y2K issue in your committees and in your home states.

Robert F. Bennett
Chairman

Christopher J. Dodd
Vice Chairman

Contents

Executive Summary

The Committee has found that the most frustrating aspect of addressing the Year 2000 (Y2K) problem is sorting fact from fiction. Reports from even the most reputable news sources fall prey to polarizing forces—either overemphasizing a handful of Y2K survivalists, or downplaying the event as a hoax designed to sell information technology equipment.

The Internet surges with rumors of massive Y2K test failures that turn out to be gross misstatements, while image-sensitive corporations downplay real Y2K problems. The good news is that talk of the death of civilization, to borrow from Mark Twain, has been greatly exaggerated. The bad news is that Committee research has concluded that the Y2K problem is very real and that Y2K risk management efforts must be increased to avert serious disruptions.

Y2K is about more than the failure of an individual's personal computer or an incorrect date in a spreadsheet. As one examines the multiple layers of systems and technologies that support our everyday lives, the potential Y2K problems increase exponentially. The interdependent nature of technology systems makes the severity of possible disruptions difficult to predict. Adding to the confusion, there are still very few overall Y2K technology compliance assessments of infrastructure or industry sectors. Consequently, the fundamental questions of risk and personal preparedness cannot be answered at this time.

On the positive side, Y2K awareness is growing. In the past year, both public and private institutions have doubled their efforts to find, evaluate, and address Y2K risk exposure. The Committee has seen a significant amount of progress since its inception. However, Senate hearings, interviews, and research have not produced convincing evidence that the Y2K problem is well in hand.

The biggest Y2K impact may occur internationally. While the U.S. should have started its Y2K preparations earlier, worldwide preparations generally lag even further behind.

Overall Observations

Many organizations critical to Americans' safety and well-being are still not fully engaged in finding a solution.

For example, over 90% of doctors' offices and 50% of small- and medium-sized businesses have yet to address the problem. Larger firms have, in general, grasped how a Y2K failure could severely impact their businesses and are taking steps to remedy the problem. Smaller firms remain more focused on what they perceive as more immediate concerns, which in many cases do not include Y2K.

Most affected industries and organizations started Y2K remediation too late.

As a result, many organizations must exercise "triage"—focusing on what is critical to sustain the life of the enterprise as opposed to finding long-term solutions.

Self-reporting has yielded unreliable assessments for most industry sectors. With few exceptions, disclosure of Y2K compliance is poor.

Analogous to letting students grade their own tests, self-reporting offers data of varying reliability. Nonetheless, it has become the standard in both private industry and government. Industry surveys are currently the most widely utilized tool to measure compliance. Unfortunately, the results of many surveys have been kept from public and Special Committee view (see "Transportation" in this report). Despite an SEC rule requiring Y2K disclosure of public corporations, companies are reluctant to report poor compliance levels.

Fear of litigation and loss of competitive advantage are the most commonly cited reasons for bare-bones disclosure.

Although sharing Y2K data could save time in companies' remediation and contingency planning efforts, such cooperation has not been forthcoming. To encourage greater disclosure, the Committee spearheaded a bipartisan effort that passed the Year 2000 Information Readiness and Disclosure Act (S.2392) and introduced the CRASH Protection Act (S.1518). The Year 2000 Information Readiness and Disclosure Act provided a basic level of protection for Y2K statements made in good faith. The CRASH Protection Act pressured the SEC to require more meaningful Y2K corporate disclosure to shareholders.

More legislation may be necessary to address Y2K litigation. Some liability cost projections are as high as $1 trillion. Serious doubts exist as to whether or not the present judicial system could handle a potentially monstrous wave of litigation.

The Committee plans to address certain key sectors in 1999 where there has been extreme reluctance to disclose Y2K compliance.

National emergency and security planning for Y2K-related systems failures is just beginning.

FEMA contingency plans are in draft form, but there is no national, strategic plan to assure that critical infrastructures will continue to function.

This is partially due to varying levels of state and local government preparedness. State and local governments represent the first line of defense in emergency situations, and emergency planning is difficult without their full involvement. A recent

Labor Department report stated that several states are lagging in specific Y2K system repairs relating to federally funded programs.

Leadership at the highest levels is lacking.

A misconception pervades corporate boardrooms that Y2K is strictly a technical problem that does not warrant executive attention. Some government sectors lack clear directives and policies on Y2K.

Sector Assessments

Since its establishment in April 1998, the Special Committee has held nine hearings on seven critical economic sectors:

- Utilities
- Healthcare
- Telecommunications
- Transportation
- Financial institutions
- Government
- General business

The eighth sector, Litigation, will be addressed in early 1999.

The Committee plans to revisit each of the sectors in 1999, with emphasis on litigation and the addition of international concerns to the list of critical sectors. The Committee will assess the nation's progress toward Y2K compliance and pinpoint problem areas. The Committee will also continue to provide recommendations to Congress for legislative action.

Utilities

While some compliance efforts are behind, the utility industry as a whole is configured to handle interruptions, blackouts, and natural disasters. A prolonged, nationwide blackout is not likely to occur. However, local and regional outages remain a distinct possibility depending upon the overall preparedness of the individual electric utility serving a given area.

The nation's electric power industry comprises 3,200 independent utilities. Overall remediation of the electric power industry is slow. According to NERC, only about 50% of the utilities had completed Y2K remediation as of December 1998. Failure of some parts of the electric industry's system is likely, but the Committee does not expect the integrity of the overall power grid to be compromised. Of greatest concern are approximately 1,000 small, rural electric utilities that may not have the resources to devote to Y2K compliance.

Compliance among oil and natural gas utilities is also progressing slowly. A survey by the Committee, while limited in scope, indicates a lack of contingency planning, overly optimistic assertions that compliance will be complete, and a lack of knowledge about suppliers' Y2K status.

Healthcare

The healthcare industry lags significantly in its Y2K preparations compared to other sectors. Because of limited resources and lack of awareness, rural and inner-city hospitals have particularly high Y2K risk exposure.

Healthcare is the nation's single largest industry, generating $1.5 trillion annually. There are 6,000 hospitals, 800,000 doctors and 50,000 nursing homes, as well as hundreds of biomedical equipment manufacturers and suppliers of blood, drugs, linens and bandages—and healthcare insurers—that may be unprepared for the year 2000.

According to a report by the Gartner Group, 64% of hospitals—primarily smaller hospitals—have no plans to test their Y2K remediation efforts. In addition, 90% of physicians' offices are unaware of their Y2K exposure. Struggling compliance efforts by HCFA (the agency that oversees Medicare) and unaddressed concerns about medical devices are major road-blocks to the industry's Y2K readiness.

Telecommunications

A massive industry-wide effort is underway to assess the impact of Y2K on telecommunications. The initial interoperability testing indicates that the U.S. communications will transition without significant problems. Currently, more than 80% of public network systems have been tested and are considered compliant.

The telecommunications industry has spent billions on Y2K fixes and should have 99% of access lines in compliance by the fall of 1999. Currently, industry and government are working together to coordinate contingency plans in case there are failures. Industry in U.S. and overseas has established warning networks to alert each other of Y2K problems.

Transportation

The transportation sector is the linchpin for just-in-time inventory management across most every sector, from healthcare supplies to food. The Y2K readiness of this sector is critical to our global economy. Planes will not fall out of the sky, but disruption of flights and global trade between some areas and countries may occur.

On average, the nation's 670 domestic airports started Y2K compliance too late. The Federal Aviation Agency has made great strides in the past year, but remains at risk. The situation with international air traffic control and airports is much more severe. The maritime shipping industry has not moved aggressively toward compliance. Public transit could be seriously disrupted.

Finance

ATMs are expected to function correctly and banks should have adequate cash to meet consumer demand, based on a Federal Reserve estimate that each American household will withdraw an *average of $500. The securities industry has responded well to its internal Y2K issues and has undertaken expansive testing. However, fund managers and brokers have only recently started to consider the implication of corporate Y2K vulnerability on investment decisions.*

The financial services sector ranks ahead of nearly all other industries in its remediation and testing efforts. Legislation in Congress and action by the Committee have led to legal requirements on broker-dealers and publicly traded companies to disclose compliance information.

Federal regulators have made considerable progress in tracking compliance among banks, thrifts and credit unions, of which 95% have received satisfactory government ratings.

Government
Several state and many local governments lag in Y2K remediation, raising the risk of service disruption. The federal government will spend in excess of $7.5 billion and will not be able to renovate, test, and implement all of its mission critical systems in time. However, wholesale failure of federal government services is not likely to occur.

The Committee's work in this sector includes national emergency planning as well as federal, state, and local government preparedness. After a late start, FEMA is now engaged in national emergency planning in the event of major and minor Y2K disruptions.

State and local governments vary widely in their Y2K preparations. Several states are not prepared to deliver critical services such as benefit payments. Of greatest concern to the Committee is the ability of local communities to provide 911 and emergency services.

The federal government also varies widely in its Y2K preparations. The Social Security Administration started early and is prepared, while other agencies, like the Department of Defense, are lagging. To its credit, the federal government publicly displays its Y2K status through quarterly and monthly reports to the Office of Management and Budget.

General Business

In general, large companies have dealt well with the Y2K problem, due to greater resources. Very small businesses may survive using manual processes until Y2K problems are remediated. However, many small- and medium-sized businesses are extremely unprepared for Y2K disruptions. One survey shows that more than 40% of 14 million small businesses do not plan to take any action.

The heavily regulated insurance, investment services, and banking industries are furthest ahead in their efforts: healthcare, oil, education, agriculture, farming, food processing, and the construction industries are lagging behind. The cost to regain lost operational capability for any mission critical failure will range from $20,000 to $3.5 million, with an average of 3 to 15 days necessary to regain lost functions.

Litigation

The prospect of litigation arising from Y2K-related failures has shadowed the Committee's work from the very beginning. Some estimates project litigation costs in excess of $1 trillion. The Committee plans to hold hearings and work closely with the Judiciary and Commerce Committees to make legislative proposals in this area.

International

Several U.S. trading partners are severely behind in their Y2K remediation efforts. For example, the Gartner Group estimates that Venezuela and Saudi Arabia (two of the largest U.S. oil importers) are 12 to 18 months behind the U.S. in their Y2K remediation efforts.

The Committee is greatly concerned about the international Y2K picture. The U.S. is dependent on a healthy global economy. It is in the interest of the U.S. to encourage Y2K remediation worldwide.

The challenges posed by the Y2K problem are numerous and daunting. The Special Committee conducted extensive research and held numerous hearings in 1998, but still cannot conclusively determine how extensive the Y2K disruptions will be. The Committee has no data to suggest that the United States will experience nation-wide social or economic collapse, but the Committee believes that some disruptions will occur, and that in some cases Y2K disruptions may be significant. The international situation may be even more tumultuous.

There are reasonable steps individuals may take to prepare for the Year 2000. Consumers are urged to keep copies of financial statements and ask local banks what efforts are being made toward Y2K compliance. Individuals should research companies' compliance levels before making investment decisions. The Y2K problem has been likened to a winter storm, with the implication that similar preparation is appropriate. Americans should prepare for Y2K based on facts and reasonable predictions about the problem's effects on vital services.

Introduction

The Year 2000 (Y2K) technology problem started as an innocuous short-term solution to the oppressively high cost of computer memory in the 1950s and 1960s. Programmers expected that the problems created by the limited, two-digit method of date storage would solve themselves as companies, governments and other computer-owners updated their hardware and software. Fifty years after the introduction of the computer, the Y2K problem has the potential to develop into a worldwide crisis. Two common human failings contributed to the crisis—the tendency to follow a path of least resistance and the reluctance to champion difficult and complex issues. The Y2K problem does not have to be a story of failure, however. If addressed successfully, Y2K may encourage political and corporate leaders to better understand and protect the critical infrastructure.

Fifty years after the birth of the computer, Y2K has developed into a worldwide collective crisis.

As memory costs fell dramatically, software writers and hardware manufacturers did not immediately expand date variables. Newer versions of hardware and software needed to interface with older versions. While some programs were modified so that a new system could accept four-digit years and still exchange information with two-digit based systems, the extra effort required slowed the changeover process. Additionally, the equipment that earlier computer experts predicted would fall into obsolescence long before 2000 survived through layers of programming updates and modifications. Instead of solving itself, the Y2K problem self-propagated around the globe.

Just as programmers found it easy to follow the tradition of using a two-digit date field, management and leadership have found it easy to defer addressing the Y2K problem. Y2K competes poorly against issues such as trade agreements, military operations, market share and product development. It lacks familiarity, and in a results-driven economy, Y2K remediation costs are difficult to justify to taxpayers or shareholders. Additionally, few wished to be associated with the potential repercussions of a failed Y2K remediation attempt.

Y2K, as the first challenge of the information age, must leave a legacy of increased awareness and appreciation of information technology's role in social and economic advancement.

At the heart of the problem lies a serious disconnect between those who use technology and those who create it. On a worldwide scale, leaders of corporations and countries are struggling to understand the Y2K problem. In the process, they are receiving a crash course in the fragile mechanics of information technology.

The Committee feels strongly that Y2K, as the first widespread challenge of the information age, must leave a legacy of increased awareness and appreciation of information technology's role in social and economic advancement.

Understanding the Problem

The goal of this section is to provide background on the Y2K problem and answer common Y2K questions.

What is the Year 2000 computer technology problem?

The phrases the "Year 2000 Computer Technology Problem," the "Millennium Bug," the "Century Date Change," or simply, "Y2K"[1] all refer to the same problem—a defect that exists in millions of computer programs worldwide that causes erroneous handling of date (i.e., day, month and year) information if not corrected. The effect of the Y2K flaw on computer systems is not easily predictable. It may bring a computer to a crashing halt. It may cause the computer to generate obviously incorrect outputs. Or alternatively, it could allow the computer to produce invalid data that will not be detected until much later, forcing users to correct a range of accumulated errors while searching for the source of the problem.

Why is two digit notation defective?

To save memory in the early days of computing, programmers represented four-digit years with only two digits. For instance, 1968 or 1974 would be stored and processed as 68 and 74, respectively. The number 19, indicating years in the 1900s, was implied, much as personal checks once had the number 19 preprinted on the dateline.

This worked smoothly until users started to input dates occurring after December 31, 1999. Computers ran into problems when required to calculate a number based on the difference in two dates, such as the interest due on a mortgage loan. Computers continued to assume that the prefix 19 was implied, so dates such as 00 or 01 were treated as 1900 or 1901. Consequently, computers could not correctly calculate the difference between a year in the 20th century and a year in the 21st century.

For example, we know that the time between July 1, 1998, and July 1, 2005 is exactly 7 years. However, a computer with a Y2K problem could calculate an answer of either 93 years or -7 years, depending on the specific program. Calculations that used either of these results would be in error and may themselves cause subsequent problems.

Another Y2K problem occurs in the storage of information. Many kinds of data are organized and processed by date, such as driver's license records and credit card accounts. Computers have had problems processing credit cards that have expiration dates after December 1999. Due to two-digit dating, computers have thought that cards expiring in 2000 or later had expired almost a century ago.

What is the scope of Y2K problems?

The Y2K problem affects two general classes of equipment. The first class comprises business systems or mainframe systems. These computers perform a variety of data-intensive calculations—balancing accounts, making payments, tracking inventory, ordering goods, managing personnel, scheduling resources, etc. The second class of equipment has several common names, including embedded chips, embedded processors and embedded control systems. Many aspects of modern society rely on microchip-enhanced technology to control or augment operations. Examples are ubiquitous. Automatic teller machines, toll collection systems, security and fire detection systems, oil and gas pipelines, consumer electronics, transportation vehicles, manufacturing process controllers, military systems, medical devices and telecommunications equipment all depend on embedded chip-technology.

Y2K related failures in business systems will generally cause an enterprise to lose partial or complete control of critical processes. In the private sector, loss of business systems means that a company may have difficulty managing its finances, making or receiving payments and tracking inventory, orders, production or deliveries. In the public sector, government organizations may be severely hindered in performing basic functions such as paying retirement and medical benefits, maintaining military readiness, responding to state and local emergencies, controlling air traffic, collecting taxes and customs and coordinating law enforcement efforts.

Y2K problems in embedded systems have the potential to affect public health and safety. Problems that need to be fixed have already been detected in medical treatment devices, water and electricity distribution and control systems, airport runway lighting and building security systems.[2] Other suspect areas are pipeline control systems and chemical and pharmaceutical manufacturing processes.

How was the Y2K mistake made?

Several factors explain the creation of the Y2K problem. In the early days of computers, computer memory was very expensive. In the IBM 7094 of the early 1960s, core memory cost around $1 per byte. Today's semiconductor memory costs around $1 per million bytes. Thus, there was a very strong economic incentive to minimize the amount of memory needed to store a program and its data in the computer's memory.

Additionally, early computer programming was highly time-consuming. Programs and data were recorded and entered into computers via 80 column punch cards. Each of the 80 columns could contain exactly one byte of information, which corresponded to one of the four digits needed to represent a year. The cumbersome nature of punched cards encouraged using as few of them as possible.

Although programmers and managers knew they had built software with latent defects in it, no one thought that software written in the 60s and 70s would survive to the Year 2000. Compounding the problem, newer software had to interface and share data with the older software. Although the new software could have handled dates internally in four digit formats and swapped data in two digit formats with the older software, to do so added complexity and hence added cost to new software. The net result was that the two-digit standard for representing years continued much longer than anyone would have guessed.

When will Y2K problems start?

Y2K problems have already surfaced in many places. Cap Gemini, a technology consulting firm, reported that as of December 1997, 7% of a group of 128 large U.S. companies had experienced Y2K related problems.[3] By March 1998, that number leaped to 37%. The Gartner Group, an information technology research company, has developed a model to predict the rate of occurrence of Y2K problems. This prediction is based on data collected quarterly from over 15,000 firms and government organizations in 87 countries. Gartner estimates a rapid increase in problems in 1999 with a peak sometime after January 1, 2000. Problem occurrences will drop off after 2000, but will still occur for another 3 to 5 years at a lower level. Finally, the Information Technology Association of America has reported that about half the major corporations in America have already experienced some form of Y2K disruption as of March 25, 1998.[4]

How can we fix Y2K and how long will it take?

It is beyond the scope of this report to cover the technical nuances of these various solutions. However, various techniques are briefly described in Appendix III.

How much are Y2K fixes going to cost?

There is no generally agreed upon answer to this question. The Gartner Group's estimate of $600 billion worldwide is a frequently cited number. Another number from a reputable source is that of Capers Jones, Software Productivity Research, Inc. of Burlington, MA. Jones' worldwide estimate is over $1.6 trillion.[5] Part of the difference is that Jones' estimate includes over $300 billion for litigation and damages but Gartner's does not. A sense of the scale of the cost can be gained from looking at the Y2K costs of six multinational financial services institutions; Citicorp, General Motors, Bank America, Credit Suisse Group, Chase Manhattan and J.P. Morgan. These six institutions have collectively estimated their Y2K costs to be over $2.4 billion. Additionally, the estimated cost of Y2K repairs is increasing, as shown in figure 1.

Can't we develop an easy Y2K fix?

Popular sentiment suggests that a technological quick fix will appear just in time to kill the millennium bug. So far, "quick fix"

Company	Past Est. (millions)	New Est. (millions)
Aetna	$139	$195
ATT	$300	$900
Bankers Trust	$180-$230	$220-$260
Cendant	$25	$53
Chase Manhattan	$300	$363
General Motors	$400-$500	$890
McDonald's	$8	$30
Merrill Lynch	$375	$560
Sears	$63	$143
Xerox	$116	$135

Figure 1: Y2K Repair Estimates[6]

claims have proved to be claims for a particular product that may show promise in one particular application, for example, finding where the actual dates and date processing routines are hidden in a program.

Software programs and computer hardware vary too greatly to be fixed by one solution. Currently, there are over 500 programming languages in use. A universal or broadly applicable Y2K solution would have to be compatible with many or most of these languages. Additionally, finding all the dates and date processing in an estimated 36,000,000 programs[7] is an enormous task difficult to automate.

The embedded processors pose another problem. Although the percentage of embedded chips with a Y2K problem is estimated to be relatively small, potentially millions of chips exist that may have to be replaced. Unfortunately, most of them are not readily accessible or easily modified.

Where can I learn more about the Y2K problem?

Many solid references can be found in the endnotes of this section and elsewhere in this report. An enormous amount of Y2K information resides on the Internet. However, legitimate information is buried among overstated rumors and half-truths. As with most other information derived from Internet sources, Y2K information must be verified for accuracy.

Additional information can be obtained through the Committee's website at www.senate.gov/~Y2K and the President's Council on Year 2000 Conversion's website at www.Y2K.gov.

Critical Infrastructures

Critical infrastructures can include both computerized services and physical services essential to minimum functioning of economy and government. More than abstract systems, critical infrastructures enable the average person to use an ATM, make a phone call and fly on an airline. In the past, many of these key infrastructures or sectors were separate. However, advances in information technology have caused many of these systems to be interconnected and linked through networks. The Committee has approached the critical infrastructures by examining the Y2K work occurring both vertically within specific sectors and horizontally across different interrelated sectors, such as banking and telecommunications.

Recognizing that the Y2K problem could have serious implications on the smooth functioning of our defense and economy, Senator Moynihan wrote President Clinton in July of 1996 and suggested a special Y2K commission. While Senator Moynihan's suggestion was not taken, Executive Order 13010 created the President's Commission on Critical Infrastructure Protection. The Commission was not tasked to study Y2K, but it recognized the potential for the Y2K problem to cause long-term problems in the infrastructures. Due to late starts, many organizations have contracted out work on sensitive systems. In some cases, organizations are sending code overseas to foreign firms. The correction of code overseas could lead to increased incidents of corporate espionage and intentional cyber disruptions. The broad scope of Y2K corrections could allow an adversary to build an exceptional understanding of sensitive systems thus enabling it to "design a subtle or comprehensive attack" against critical systems.[8]

The question is not will there be disruptions, but how severe the disruptions will be.

It is absolutely vital that the owners, operators and regulators of the nation's critical systems continue to be aware that Y2K may provide an opportunity for those with malicious intent. Sandia National Laboratories warned the Committee that:

"Thinking that we will be so preoccupied with Y2K that we would not notice deliberate malicious intent, terrorists, hackers and other criminals might see Y2K as a prime opportunity to attack pieces of our infrastructure. Or they might use Y2K-induced infrastructure failures as cover for theft, arson, bombings, etc. We must be watchful of such groups in the months leading up to Y2K and we must be especially careful when monitoring the crisis as it occurs to discern deliberate intent."[9]

Current national security and emergency preparedness policies are not designed for the challenges of the information age. The U.S. needs a system or process whereby the government can coordinate responses with the privately owned and operated critical infrastructures. We must build the broad based contingency plans necessary to ensure that the national security and emergency preparedness posture of the U.S. is not compromised by Y2K. The U.S. must remain ready to mitigate the (economic, emergency or security) effects that could be caused by Y2K.

Y2K is an opportunity to educate ourselves first hand about the nature of 21st century threats. Technology has provided the

U.S. with many advantages, but it also creates many new vulnerabilities. Recognizing shifts in the technological topography of the nation requires vision. Reverting to a world without microchips or technology-dependent systems is not only undesirable, but also impossible. Instead, we, as a nation and as individuals, need to consider carefully our reliance on information technology and the consequences of interconnectivity, and work to protect that which we have so long taken for granted.

Formation of the Special Committee

Senator Robert Bennett first identified the Year 2000 as an issue for the legislative agenda in 1996 as the Senate organized for the 105th Congress. He shared his concerns with Senator Alfonse D'Amato, Chairman of the Senate Banking Committee, who urged Senator Bennett to take up the issue in his new role as Chairman of the Subcommittee on Financial Services and Technology.

The Subcommittee naturally focused its first efforts on the regulators' efforts to ensure Y2K compliance. In February 1997 and again in April 1997, Senators D'Amato and Bennett requested information on Y2K preparations from the following financial regulatory agencies:

- The Federal Reserve Board (FRB)
- The Federal Deposit Insurance Corporation (FDIC)
- The Office of Thrift Supervision (OTS)
- The National Credit Union Administration (NCUA)
- The Office of the Comptroller of the Currency (OCC)
- The Securities and Exchange Commission (SEC)

Shortly after the Committee inquiry, the Federal Financial Institutions Examination Council (FFIEC), an inter agency body made up of FRB, FDIC, OTS, NCUA and OCC, issued guidelines for the financial institutions and federal examiners to focus on issues they must address to avoid major service disruptions due to Y2K.[10]

Individual agency responses revealed varying degrees of readiness. The SEC's response detailed extensive plans for remediation and testing, while other agencies demonstrated little more than a general awareness and initial response to the problem. Many of the regulatory agencies deferred to statements published by FFIEC without providing any substantive information about their own progress. These results prompted Senator Bennett to conduct the first hearing on financial services and the Year 2000 on July 10, 1997.

At the end of the first hearing, Senator Christopher Dodd quickly recognized the importance of the Y2K issue and voiced his support for additional hearings on Y2K. The Subcommittee held another eight hearings to investigate the scope and severity of the Y2K problem and to prompt action in the financial community.

On November 10, 1997, Senator Bennett introduced the Computer Remediation and Shareholder Protection Act of 1997 (CRASH Protection Act), which required the Securities and Exchange Commission to increase its disclosure regulations relative to Y2K readiness. With the threat of the CRASH Protection Act looming, the SEC redoubled its efforts to raise awareness of Y2K implications.

Also in November 1997, Senator Bennett wrote President Clinton to express concern over a lack of national leadership in the Y2K arena. The Senator suggested the appointment of a Y2K "czar" to oversee the Y2K compliance of the federal government and initiate a public-private Y2K action. Three months later, President Clinton issued Executive Order 13073, creating the President's Council on Year 2000 Conversion. Subsequently, John Koskinen was tapped to chair the new council.

During these events, the Subcommittee struggled to reach industries outside of banking. SEC disclosures provided a tool, albeit blunt, to raise Y2K awareness and planning within public companies. Despite staff bulletins emphasizing the application of disclosure law to the Y2K issue, the level of information disclosed in March 1998 was disappointingly low. Indeed, some companies overlooked Y2K entirely under the premise that Y2K did not present a material threat to their businesses. Meanwhile, off-the-record discussions with Subcommittee staff suggested that many corporations preferred to incur SEC fines rather than a drop in their stock prices. The Subcommittee invited the SEC to a June 1998 hearing, which led to additional guidance in the form of an interpretive release on Y2K disclosure. However, the point was made that the Subcommittee on Financial Services and Technology simply did not provide the scope necessary to adequately address the breadth and depth of the Y2K problem.

Voicing this concern, Senators Bennett and Dodd met with the Senate leadership. Senate Majority Leader Trent Lott recognized the importance of Senate leadership in the Y2K arena and with the assistance of Minority Leader Tom Daschle, cleared the way for the creation of the Special Committee on the Year 2000 Technology Problem.

On April 2, 1998, the U.S. Senate unanimously voted to establish a new committee to address the Y2K technology problem. The Special Committee on the Year 2000 Technology Problem was authorized through February 29, 2000. The Majority Leader named Senator Bennett to serve as its Chairman. Committee membership included:

- Vice-Chairman Senator Christopher Dodd
  (D-Connecticut)
- Senator Jon Kyl (R-Arizona)
- Senator Susan Collins (R-Maine)
- Senator Gordon Smith (R-Oregon)
- Senator Daniel Patrick Moynihan (D-New York)
- Senator Jeff Bingaman (D-New Mexico
- Senator Ted Stevens (R-Alaska) *ex-officio*
- Senator Robert Byrd (D-West Virginia) *ex-officio*

Because the Committee does not have legislative authority, each of the members was carefully selected based on membership on other committees, such as Judiciary, Armed Services and Government Affairs.

According to the legislation that created it, the Senate Special Committee on the Year 2000 Technology Problem will exist until February 29, 2000, after which it will permanently disband.

Utilities

The Committee has taken a broad-based approach to utilities—aggregating electrical power, gas and oil, and water (drinking and wastewater) in this sector. Telecommunications—is discussed separately in another section of this report.

Electric Utilities

One of the most often asked questions concerning Y2K is, "Will the lights stay on?" In general, the answer is yes. However, progress in assessing, remediating, and testing is insufficient to answer this question absolutely. As with other sectors, some general conclusions can be drawn. First, the large corporations, or bulk power producers, are spending vast resources to get the Y2K problem under control. However, each of the 3,200 electric utilities is at a different stage of remediation, and many may experience problems. All of the evidence seems to indicate that there

Electrical power is key to every other sector: The lights must stay on!

may be isolated and diverse electrical outages across the country. The questions now are: Where will they occur, how long will they last, and will they be significant enough to affect the overall grid?

The Committee made electric utilities its top priority because of its critical importance to everything else—without electric power little else will work. As a result, the status of electric power is the number one concern for all other sectors.

Overview

There are about 3,200 independent electric utilities in the United States including about

- 250 investor-owned or private utilities,
- 10 government-owned utilities,
- 2,000 other publicly owned utilities, and
- 900 cooperatives.

Nearly 80% of the nation's power generation comes from the 250 investor-owned public utilities. The federal government generates another 10% of the nation's power, primarily through large facilities such as the Tennessee Valley Authority and the Bonneville Power Authority. There are another 2,000 non-utilities, or privately owned entities, that generate power for their own use and/or for sale to utilities and others.

Electric power is generated from the following sources:

- 51% by coal
- 20% by nuclear energy
- 15% by gas
- 10% by hydro and
- 4% by other sources.

The approximately 900 cooperatives generally have limited power-generation capacity and focus primarily on distribution systems.

The electric power industry is complex and highly automated. It is made up of an interconnected network of generation plants (nuclear, fossil fuel, gas, hydro, etc.), transmission lines (commonly referred to as the "grid"), and distribution facilities. There are three independent interconnections or grids that provide electricity to every household and company in North America.

In its simplest form, each of these grids operates as a single machine, constantly making adjustments to balance the amount of power being generated with the amount being used. These adjustments are critical because electric power cannot be stored. Too much power could literally melt transmission and distribution lines; too little power could result in brown outs.

It takes a high degree of automation to operate the grid. On one hand, it is this high degree of interconnectedness that gives the system its unprecedented reliability and efficiency. On the other hand, the interconnectedness makes the grid fragile and susceptible to Y2K disruptions. An outage in one part of the grid can cascade causing ripple effects on other parts of the grid. For example, a generation plant could go out in Maine, affecting power in Florida.

The basic structure of an electric power transmission and distribution system consists of a generating system, a transmission system, a sub-transmission system, a distribution system, and a control center. Power plant generation systems may include steam turbines, diesel engines, or hydraulic turbines connected to alternators that generate AC electricity.

In most respects, the electric industry faces the same Y2K challenges as every other industry. Y2K anomalies could lead to the malfunction of software programs on mainframe computers, servers, PCs, and communications systems. Corrupted data could be passed from one application to another causing erroneous results or shutdowns. This means computer programs used for accounting, administration, billing, and other important functions could experience problems.

Of greater concern to the electric power industry are embedded computers—small electronic chips or control devices. These chips are used extensively in all parts of the electric power industry including generating plants, transmission lines, distribution systems, and power control systems. Even though only a small number of these embedded devices will have a Y2K problem, it is impossible to tell which ones until each chip has been checked and tested—a time consuming venture.

Making matters worse, electronic chips are generally mass-produced without knowing the ultimate application of the chip. A single circuit board can have 20–50 of these chips from various manufacturers. Because of the diversity of chip suppliers, one vendor may use a different mix of chips even within devices labeled with the same name, model number, and year. Many of these chips have built-in clocks that may experience date change anomalies associated with Y2K.

There are numerous mission critical systems essential to the production, transmission, and delivery of electric power. Y2K risks in electric power can be grouped into five areas.

1. Power Production Systems

Generating units must be able to operate through critical Y2K periods without disruption. Units that are scheduled to operate must be able to start up and deliver electricity as planned. The threat is most severe in power plants with Digital Control Systems (DCSs). Many older plants operating with analog controls may be less problematic. Numerous control and protection systems within the DCS use time-dependent algorithms, which may result in generating unit trips when encountering a Y2K anomaly. Digital controllers that have been built into station equipment, protection relays, and communications may also pose risks.

2. Energy Management Systems

There are approximately 200 bulk electric control centers in North America. From these control centers, system operators monitor and control the backbone of the electrical systems and dispatch generation to meet demand. Computer systems within these control centers use complex algorithms to manage the operations of transmission facilities and to dispatch generating units. At any moment in time, a percentage (usually 10–20%) of generating units may be on automatic control for the purpose of following load and regulating interconnection frequency. Many of the control center software applications contain built-in time clocks used to run various power system monitoring, dispatch, and control functions. Some energy management systems are dependent on time signal emissions from Global Positioning Satellites. Beyond the 200 operating centers, there are hundreds of additional control centers used to manage sub-transmission and distribution systems. These systems are typically operated using a subset of an energy management system, called Supervisory Control and Data Acquisition (SCADA).

3. Telecommunications Systems

Electric power systems are highly dependent on microwave, telephone, VHF radio, and satellite communications. If the control centers are the "brains" of the electrical grids, communications systems are the "nervous system." Telecommunications is the single most important area in which the electric systems depend on another industry. Many of the telephone, microwave, and network services used for communications in the electric industry are provided by telephone companies and other communications and network service providers. The dependency of electric supply and delivery systems on external service providers is a crucial factor in successful performance during Y2K transition periods.

4. Substation Control Systems

Throughout electric transmission and distribution systems there are substations that contain control equipment such as circuit breakers, disconnect switches, and transformers. Remote terminal units (RTUs) in substations serve as the communications hubs for the substations, allowing them to communicate with the control centers. Substations also contain most of the transmission and distribution system protection relays, which serve to operate circuit breakers to quickly isolate equipment should an electrical fault occur on a line, transformer, or other piece of equipment.

5. Distribution Systems

Distribution systems deliver electricity from the transmission network to customers. There is a lot of commonality in the types of substation equipment in distribution compared to transmission. Distribution systems have additional equipment outside substations (for example, along a distribution feeder) that may have electronic controls. Examples include reclosers (relays that open and close a feeder in rapid succession to allow a fault to clear), capacitors, voltage regulators, and special monitoring devices.

Although the five areas outlined above focus directly on the production and delivery of electricity, other support systems are essential to sustained operations of the electrical service provider. These systems have been grouped under the heading "Business Information Systems" in this report. They include among others customer service call centers, supply and inventory systems, and accounting systems.

Major Players

Several federal organizations are involved in various aspects of the electric power industry. Primary are the Department of

Energy's (DOE) whose mission is to formulate a comprehensive energy policy encompassing all national energy resources, including electricity; and the Federal Energy Regulatory Commission (FERC), an independent agency overseeing the natural gas industry, the electric utilities, non-federal hydroelectric projects, and oil pipeline transport. Other federal agencies that oversee the electric power transmission and distribution industry include

- the Nuclear Regulatory Commission (NRC),
- the Rural Utility Service (RUS),
- the Environmental Protection Agency (EPA), and
- the Securities and Exchange Commission (SEC).

At the request of DOE, the North American Electric Reliability Council (NERC)—a non-federal entity—has assumed the primary role in monitoring the overall Y2K preparedness of the electric power industry. NERC is a logical choice for this role because it is the organization most involved in keeping the lights on in North America. Formed in 1968 in response to a cascading blackout that left almost 30 million people without electricity, members are drawn from all ownership segments of the industry—investor-owned, federal, state, municipal, rural, and provincial. NERC is a nonprofit corporation composed of ten regional councils.

The members of the regional councils are electric utilities, independent power producers and electricity marketers that account for most of the electricity supplied in the United States, Canada, and Mexico.

State public utility commissions (PUCs) play the most significant role regulating the electric power industry. PUCs control the rate structure for all municipal utilities, investor-owned utilities, and rural electric cooperatives that own, maintain, or operate an electric generation, transmission, or distribution system within a state. By controlling what constitutes an allowable charge, classifying accounts, and structuring rates, the PUCs can exert significant influence over utilities. The PUCs also regulate reliability for both operational and emergency purposes, oversee territorial agreements, and resolve territorial disputes between utilities.

Other significant Y2K players in the electrical power industry include the:

- American Public Power Association (APPA)
- Electric Power Research Institute (EPRI)
- National Rural Electric Cooperative Association (NRECA)
- Edison Electric Institute (EEI)
- Nuclear Energy Institute (NEI)
- Canadian Electric Association (CEA)

Major Initiatives

The Senate Year 2000 Committee held its first hearing on energy utilities on June 12, 1998. We received testimony from Administration officials and key players in the electrical power industry including John Koskinen, Chairman, President's Council on Year 2000 Conversion; Elizabeth Moler, Deputy Secretary, DOE; Shirley Ann Jackson, Chairman, NRC; Michehl Gent, President, NERC; and Dr. Charles Siebenthal, Manager Y2K Programs, EPRI. In addition, because of the lack of data on the overall status of the electric power industry, the Committee conducted a survey of large electric and gas and oil utilities.

The Committee's survey results clearly indicated that electric utilities did not have an accurate picture of their current state of Y2K readiness. Most utilities had just begun to assess their systems and embedded devices.

John Koskinen outlined the structure of the President's Y2K Council and reported that DOE would head the electric power sector.

DOE testified that it lacked the regulatory authority to force industry compliance. DOE asked NERC for help in building an understanding of Y2K efforts in the electric power industry. NERC also assumed responsibility for surveying the industry.

APPA, where members include many state and local municipal electricity providers, is coordinating information sharing and surveys of its members, as well as smaller non-member public power utilities. APPA is assisting NERC in the industry-wide readiness review of electric distribution systems.

EPRI is focusing its Y2K program on embedded systems and the associated Y2K technical and project management issues. Over one hundred companies are participating in the EPRI information-sharing program, representing over 74 percent of the electric power consumed in North America.

EEI represents investor-owned utilities. It has established a program to address Y2K technical, regulatory, and liability issues. EEI is also assisting in the readiness review of electric distribution systems.

NRECA is coordinating Y2K readiness assessments and information sharing among its membership, which includes nearly 1,000 rural electric systems.

NEI is coordinating the assessment of Y2K readiness of U.S. nuclear facilities and is providing that information as part of the NERC surveys.

CEA is assisting NERC by coordinating efforts in Canada, particularly to address the readiness of electric distribution systems and Canadian nuclear facilities.

Assessment

At the time of the hearing, there was a lack of industry-wide survey data of the electric power industry. As a result, the Committee staff surveyed five large electric and five large gas and oil companies to obtain cursory readiness information. Figure 1 displays the result of the survey.

Company	Date Aware	Establish Formal Project	Assessment Complete	Percent Systems Mission Critical	Status of Service Providers/Vendors	Legal or Liability Concerns	Contingency Plans Complete	Contacts by Creditors	Contacts by Investors	Will You Finish In Time
1	1995	Yes	No	54	?	Yes	No	Yes	-	Yes
2	1995	Yes	Yes	5	?	Yes	No	Yes	Yes	Yes
3	1996	Yes	No	?	?	Yes	No	No	Yes	Yes
4	1992	Yes	No	30	?	Yes	No	Yes	Yes	Yes
5	1995	Yes	Yes	50	?	No	No	Yes	Yes	Yes
6	-	Yes	No	?	?	Yes	No	Yes	Yes	Yes
7	1996	Yes	No	?	?	Yes	No	Yes	Yes	Yes
8	1996	Yes	No	25	?	No	No	Yes	Yes	Yes
9	1996	Yes	No	35	?	Yes	No	Yes	Yes	Yes
10	1996	Yes	No	18	?	No	No	Yes	Yes	Yes

Figure 1: Committee Survey Results

Based on the survey results, the Committee concluded that the utilities were proceeding in the right direction, but the pace of remedial efforts was too slow and there was so much remaining to be done that there was significant cause for concern. Only two of the eight firms reported completion of assessment, making assertions of Y2K compliance by December 1999 highly suspect. Committee concern was heightened because the most difficult tasks—renovation and testing—were yet to come.

The utilities' lack of information regarding Y2K compliance of their major suppliers, vendors, and service providers created additional concerns about the utilities' assertions of readiness. The survey results raise significant levels of concern given that the firms surveyed were among the largest utilities and were dedicating many resources to Y2K (collectively over $400 million). Smaller firms with fewer resources are presumably further behind in their Y2K remediation efforts.

On September 17, 1998, three months after the Committee's hearing, NERC issued its first comprehensive report of electrical power industry readiness based on survey data collected at the end of August. It has issued two monthly updates since that time. Participation by the 200 bulk electric operating entities increased from 144 in August to 155 and 188 in the September and October surveys, respectively.

About 2,200 of the 3,000 distribution entities, i.e., the actual electric utilities, have participated in the NERC process by responding to data gathered by APPA and NRECA and providing it to the appropriate bulk electric operating entity. NERC's overall survey results are depicted in figure 2.

While the NERC surveys clearly show progress in August, September, and October, the question is whether there is sufficient time to complete Y2K remediation efforts. The data presented in the NERC report do not seem to support the optimistic tone contained in the report's executive summary. Of particular concern is that, with only a little over a year to go, 34% of the firms are operating without a written plan.

In addition, the assessment phase is only 75% complete (federal agencies are 99% complete with this phase). Remediation and testing is only 36% complete. Given that Y2K experts contend that between 40 and 70% of the total effort will be expended in testing alone, there may not be sufficient time to complete this.

The highly interconnected nature of the grids raises concern about cascading failures. This in turn obviates the need for contingency planing, particularly plans for addressing capacity

Y2K Status of Electric Power Industry

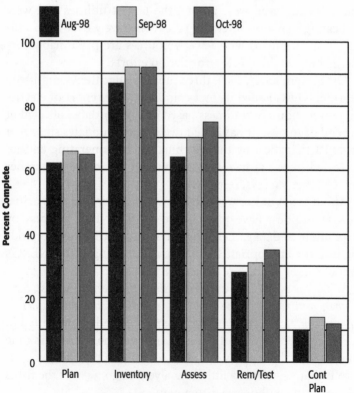

Figure 2: NERC Monthly Status Report

shortages and overages—of which only 13% of the firms surveyed have in place.

Although nuclear plants are addressed in the overall NERC study, public concern about their safety dictates that the Committee provide specific information regarding the overall Y2K preparedness of these plants. Nuclear facilities are lagging behind other electric facilities in their Y2K assessment and remediation efforts.

In general, nuclear facilities contain very old analog technology and, as a result, have fewer Y2K issues than the more digital and modern fossil fuel facilities. Nevertheless, assessments to date have revealed varying degrees of problems in areas such as plant process control, feed water monitoring, refueling, turbine control, and building security and access control.

While these problems should not affect plant safety, they could cause serious electricity production problems. While NRC has legal authority only to address plant safety issues, it is working closely with NEI to assess nuclear plants. NRC plans detailed Y2K assessments of 12 of the nearly 70 nuclear facilities. It has completed assessments on six of these plants, and has issued reports on the first three. These reports are publicly available on NRC's web site.

Concerns

- While complete power grid failure and prolonged blackout is highly unlikely, failure of at least some parts of the electric power industry, e.g., local or regional outages, is possible. The 3,200 electric utilities are at various stages of remediation. The likelihood of outages in a given area is directly related to the overall preparedness of the individual electric utility serving that area.
- Overall Y2K remediation progress has been slow due to the industry's late start, the complexity of the power grids, and the magnitude of the problems. As a result,

power companies must step up their efforts, and develop workable contingency plans in the event their best efforts fall short.

- The interconnectivity of the electric generation and transmission entities making up the grids is a strength and a weakness. On the one hand, interconnectivity provides flexibility in that electricity can be routed around trouble spots. On the other hand, outages in one part of the grid could affect power in other parts of the grid. There are no comprehensive studies concerning the number of entities that would have to fail to put the entire grid at risk, but some experts suggest that it may be a very small percentage if in key locations.

- The interrelationship of the electric power sector with other sectors it depends on—telecommunications, natural gas and oil supplies and pipelines, and rail transportation for coal supplies—requires close coordination. There are signs that this coordination is beginning, but efforts need to be stepped up so that the electric utilities can engage in more meaningful contingency planning.

- The bulk power entities are spending large amounts of money on Y2K remediation and most are making good progress. Of greater concern are some of the smaller and medium-sized distribution entities that may not have sufficient resources to devote to the problem. Each is an essential link to the overall success of the industry.

- State public utility commissioners must play an active role in ensuring that the electrical utilities under their purview are taking appropriate Y2K remediation, risk reduction, and contingency planning actions. In addition, they should keep the public informed about the status of the utilities.

- Nuclear plants are at various stages of Y2K remediation. Some have only recently begun to assess the systems within their plants. Even if for no other reason than to allay public concern, NRC needs to expand its detailed Y2K assessments to include all nuclear plants. In addition, not withstanding the NRC charter of addressing safety issues only, it needs to broaden the scope of its Y2K assessments to include operational issues as well.

- The electric industry is in the middle of a major restructuring to introduce wholesale and retail competition for electricity. Attention has been on competing in the marketplace, cutting costs, mergers, reorganizations, and survival. The industry must find a way to ensure that all of this restructuring activity does not interfere with the more immediate concerns of timely Y2K remediation.

Oil & Gas Utilities

This sector covers both oil products and natural gas; however, the Committee's hearing focused primarily on natural gas as the principal source of residential heating. Oil provides about 40 percent of the energy Americans consume, including home heating. In addition, about 60 million American homes and businesses use natural gas for heating, cooking, and other applications.

Gas and oil utilities face a variety of Y2K problems in their administrative systems, as well as the microprocessors or computer chips embedded in the production, transportation and distribution systems used in this industry. Survey results published by the Federal Energy Regulatory Commission (FERC) in September 1998 show that this industry, like many others, started its Y2K efforts late.

According to the survey, most of the critical systems in this industry are still in the inventory and assessment phase, leaving little time for the more difficult phases of Y2K remediation and testing. As a result, the industry is not likely to complete repairs of all of its system in time, which in turn means that possible disruptions in the production, transportation, and distribution of gas and oil are possible.

Automation and, thus, Y2K concerns are prevalent throughout both the gas and oil industries. FERC published a generic diagram that maps out the elements of gas and oil production, transmission, and distribution that must be checked for Y2K problems.

Note: This year, the Committee plans to increase attention to the oil industry, particularly the international Y2K implications on oil imports. The U.S. gets nearly 50 percent of its oil from imports, and several key oil producing countries are behind in their Y2K remediation efforts. If these countries are unable to sustain the level of imports because of Y2K failures in the pumping, refining, or transportation of crude oil, the implications on the price of gasoline may be significant.

Overview

Nearly all Americans rely on oil and gas in their everyday lives. Oil provides about 40 percent of the energy Americans consume. Besides the obvious gasoline, diesel fuel, and home heating oil, petroleum products are used in everything from toothpaste to raincoats. A barrel of crude oil (42 gallons) is refined into

Product	Gallons*
Gasoline	19.5
Fuel oil	9.2
Jet fuel	4.1
Residual fuel	2.3
Liquefied gas	1.9
Still gas	1.9
Coke	1.8
Asphalt	1.3
Petrochemicals	1.2
Lubricants	0.5
Kerosene	0.2
Other	0.3

*Totals more than 42 gallons due to processing gains.

Almost 60 million American homes and businesses use natural gas for heating, hot water, cooking and other applications. Natural gas comes through a 1.3 million-mile underground system. The U.S. has about 58,000 miles of gathering lines in the gas production areas, 260,000 miles of long-distance pipelines, and nearly 1 million miles of distribution lines operated by local gas utilities that must all be checked for Y2K problems.

Thousands of embedded systems in millions of miles of pipelines all must be checked and, if necessary, replaced. Vulnerable systems include distributed control systems, programmable logic controllers, digital recorders, control stations, recorders, meters, meter reading and calibration software, and SCADA. PC-based applications such as control and work management software within a utility may also possess Y2K vulnerability. Any date-dependent application, system or component may experience problems that result in complete system or station shut-down.

The President's Council on Year 2000 Conversion assigned FERC responsibility for the gas and oil sector. Other federal agencies involved in this sector include the Department of Energy, the Department of Transportation (pipelines are a form of interstate transportation), the Department of the Interior, and the General Services Administration.

Trade associations representing the various gas and oil entities are also playing a key role in Y2K remediation efforts for this industry.[1]

Major Initiatives

The Committee's energy utility hearing was held on June 12, 1998. As described in the previous section, both electric utilities and oil and gas utilities were addressed. Gas and oil witnesses included, the Honorable James Hoecker, Chairman, FERC, Mr. James Rubright, Executive Vice President, Sonat, Inc.

representing INGAA, and Gary Gardner, Chief Information Officer, AGA, and Lou Marcoccia, energy industry consultant.

The hearing better defined the Y2K problem in the gas and oil sector, heightened awareness, and mobilized an industry that was not yet fully engaged in addressing the Y2K problem.

In his testimony, Mr. Hoecker indicated that the Y2K status of the gas and oil industry is essentially unknown. He was especially concerned about small and medium sized companies and focused on the need for the gas and oil industry to share Y2K testing and compliance information. He indicated that Y2K readiness information might be difficult to obtain because of fear that the information may be commercially sensitive, that certain liability issues may arise, or that collaboration on this problem may expose companies to anti-trust actions.

The Committee was key to passing Y2K information disclosure legislation and obtaining clarification from the Justice Department to exempt Y2K information exchange from anti-trust laws. Mr. Hoecker also suggested that a Y2K database be established. API has since set up such a database.

Mr. Rubright, representing the interstate gas pipeline companies, highlighted the extensive use of embedded chips in the computerized devices instrumental to the operation and monitoring of gas and oil pipelines. According to him, most pipeline companies contend they will be Y2K ready by October 1999, but are concerned over both upstream and downstream suppliers, as well as utilities and telecommunications providers on which they rely. He also expressed concern over litigation risks, the large number of congressional electronic commerce initiatives, and anti-trust issues.

Mr. Gardner, representing gas utilities, focused on the complexity of gas distribution systems. He indicated that a gas utility will typically have between 50 and 100 systems with embedded processing located in such areas as storage fields, gas control and management operations, metering and facilities, and SCADA systems. His industry's experience suggests that the process of identifying, replacing or upgrading, and testing takes 12 to 18 months to complete.

The Committee's hearing was instrumental in motivating the President's Council on Y2K Conversion to create an oil and gas working group. The kick-off meeting for the oil and gas group was held at FERC in June 1998.

FERC has held subsequent meetings on July 14, 1998, September 3, 1998, and November 13, 1998. Minutes of the Oil and Gas Working Group meetings and other proceedings and events are publicly available on FERC's website.

API, a national trade association representing all phases of the oil and gas industry, provides direct assistance to FERC in managing the working group. In 1997, the API formed a Year 2000 Task Force to facilitate Y2K readiness across the petroleum industry. The API Year 2000 Task Force currently represents over 50 industry companies and meets every 6 to 7 weeks.

One of API's primary functions is to alert and educate industry members about the potential impact of Y2K on information, process control, automation and instrumentation systems, as well as concerns about other companies in the supply chain. API has also created a database to allow companies to share information about the readiness status of computer software and hardware, telecommunications networks, process control and electrical equipment, and embedded systems used by the petroleum industry.

AGA, a trade association of almost 300 natural gas transmission, distribution, gathering and marketing companies, and 181 local natural gas utilities that deliver gas to 54 million homes and businesses, has also been actively involved in Y2K. AGA members account for more than 90 percent of natural gas delivered in the United States.

AGA sponsors business television series, joint information technology conferences, and other forums to inform its membership of Y2K solutions.

Assessment

The Committee's survey, depicted in figure 1, included both electric and gas and oil utility companies. Concerns resulting from the survey expressed in the electric utility section of this report also apply to the gas and oil utilities. Progress is slow progress, assertions that they will complete Y2K remediation efforts in time are overly optimistic, the industry lacks knowledge about suppliers' Y2K status, and contingency planning is deficient.

The Committee's survey, although limited in scope, was the only available survey at the time. Since then, FERC released its first overall assessment of the Y2K status and preparedness of the gas and oil industry on September 18, 1998. AGA in coordination with the Gas Research Institute and the Interstate Natural Gas Association of America collected and analyzed surveys of its members to assess the industry's compliance with Y2K requirements. These surveys form the basis for the FERC assessment. Assessment results are depicted in figure 3 for business systems and figure 4 for embedded systems.

The survey was sent to over 8,000 gas and oil companies. Only 638 or less than 10% responded. Although the response was disappointing, it did represent 45% of oil and gas production, 78% of refining capacity, 70% of crude and product pipeline deliveries, and 43% of U.S. service stations.

The survey asked companies to indicate the stage their companies were in for business systems and for embedded systems. This required companies to summarize information at too high a level to be meaningful. In reality, a company may have hundreds or even thousands of business and embedded systems each at a different stage of remediation. Nevertheless, the survey results are still alarming. The survey indicates that 45% of companies who responded consider themselves to be in the assessment phase or earlier for business systems, and 60% for embedded systems.

The Committee can only conclude that, despite claims to the

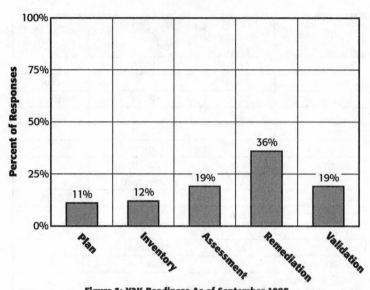

Figure 3: Y2K Readiness As of September 1998
Business Information Systems & Associated Software

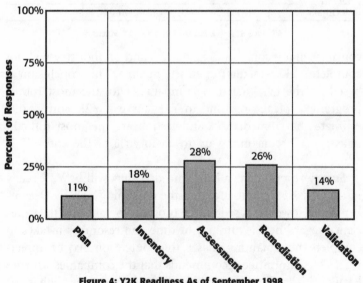

Figure 4: Y2K Readiness As of September 1998
Embedded Systems

Country	Percent U.S. Imports	Y2K Status (Months Behind U.S.)	Risk of Disruption
Venezuela	16.2	12–18	High
Canada	15.5	0–3	Low
Saudi Arabia	14.4	12–18	High
Mexico	12.9	12	Medium
Nigeria	7.3	12–18	High
Angola	4.2	Unknown	?
Colombia	3.0	12–18	High
Algeria	2.9	Unknown	?
Kuwait	2.9	12–18	High
Virgin Islands	2.9	Unknown	?
Norway	2.3	12	Medium
Iraq	2.2	Unknown	?
Gabon	2.0	Unknown	?
United Kingdom	2.0	0–3	Low
Ecuador	0.9	12–18	High
Argentina	0.9	12–18	High
All Others	7.5	Unknown	?

Figure 5: Imported Oil Country Y2K Status

contrary, many companies in the gas and oil industry will not complete Y2K remediation efforts in time. This conclusion is based on the fact that only companies with the most robust programs typically respond to Y2K surveys. Y2K consultants estimate that remediation and testing are the most difficult phases, often consuming up to 40 to 70% of the entire Y2K effort.

Survey respondents all contend that they will be Y2K ready in time—76% by June 1999 and the remaining 24% by December 1999. However, based on the progress to date, and the experience regarding the amount of time and resources it takes to complete the remaining phases, this contention may be unrealistic. The Committee recommends that the companies who are lagging this far behind, i.e., are still in the assessment phase or earlier, devote significant resources to contingency planning because they will not have sufficient time to repair and test all of their mission critical systems in the limited time remaining.

One of the biggest areas of concern for the Committee is the Y2K status of countries from which the U.S. imports oil. Nearly 50% of the oil used in the U.S. comes from foreign sources. Yet, as depicted in figure 5, many of the countries are significantly behind the U.S., and thus, have a high risk of failure. Indeed, 3 of the top 5 countries from which the U.S. imports oil are, according to the Gartner Group, 12 to 18 months behind the U.S. in their Y2K remediation efforts. This means that oil production and transportation may be at risk in these countries. Any disruption to oil imports could significantly impact oil availability and, thus, prices in the U.S. The oil industry and the federal government need to monitor this situation closely.

Concerns

- Y2K remediation in the gas and oil sector began too late and is progressing too slowly. The thousands of miles of pipeline that must be checked and repaired and the proliferation of embedded chips and processors throughout the industry's production, transportation, and distribution systems make failure of at least some mission-critical systems possible. The industry needs to step up its efforts and focus on developing contingency plans.
- The dependence of the gas and oil industry on other sectors—electric power and telecommunications—dictates better coordination with these sectors.
- While the large gas and oil companies are spending large amounts of money on Y2K remediation, the Committee is concerned about some of the smaller and medium-sized companies in this industry, including those up and down the supply chain. These small companies could be the linchpins for the overall success of this industry.

- A Y2K assessment of oil producing countries is needed to determine the likelihood that U.S. oil imports will be disrupted, and, if so, what contingency planning will be needed.

Water Utilities

Overview

Water

There are approximately 200,000 public water systems (PWSs) regulated under the Safe Drinking Water Act that serve 243 million people in the United States. The remaining population obtains their drinking water from private wells.

PWSs are defined as community water systems, non-transient, non-community, or transient systems. Approximately 60,000 of the 200,000 public water systems are classified as community water systems. A community water system provides water to the same population year round. There are 3,687 community water systems in the U.S., which serve a population of 10,000 or more, and provide water to a total of 204 million people.

Approximately 75 percent of the American public is served by large community water systems covering populations of 100,000 or more. There are over 30 community water systems serving populations in excess of one million people.

Although the community water systems collectively serve a large number of people, most community water systems serve less than 3,300 people. Many of those systems are privately owned and operated.

A transient non-community water system serves transitory customers in non-residential areas such as campgrounds, motels, and gas stations. Approximately 57 percent of public water systems are transient non-community systems. (Sources: EPA Report to Congress, EPA-810-R-93-1. September 1991, and AWWA/AMWA/NAAW 1998 Survey.)

Wastewater

Seventy-two percent of the U.S. population (190 million people) is served by centralized wastewater treatment facilities; the remainder is served by on-site systems (e.g., septic systems).

There are 16,000 wastewater treatment facilities nationwide, with operations ranging from less than 100,000 gallons per day (about 1/3 of the total number of facilities) to systems that treat over 100 million gallons per day (less than 1% of the systems).

Systems such as Prince William County, Virginia, and Independence, Missouri, treat approximately 10 million gallons of sewage a day, while the largest systems, such as those of New York or Chicago, treat approximately 1.5 billion gallons of sewage per day.

Nationwide, approximately 42 billion gallons of sewage are treated per day.

About 31% of the U.S. population is served by facilities that provide secondary treatment of waste and another 31% is served by facilities that provide better than secondary. Fifty percent of the design capacity of existing treatment plants allows for better than secondary treatment.

The remaining population is served either by plants that have no discharge or by individual on-site disposal systems.

Municipal governments own 95% of wastewater treatment facilities, either as part of a local government's public works department, or as a separate authority or utility district.

Typically, in small to medium-sized cities, the water utility and wastewater treatment systems are operated jointly. In larger cities they are usually separate operations.[2]

Major Initiatives

The Committee assessed the Y2K vulnerability of the water and wastewater, and took steps to increase awareness about Y2K issues in this vital sector of service. These include staff networking with the major water and wastewater industry association groups and the Environmental Protection Agency (EPA). The Committee also interviewed numerous industry experts, surveyed water and wastewater company Y2K preparedness, and monitored other industry surveys recently administered by the major water and wastewater industry associations.

The Committee staff has also participated with the EPA in tours of five local Washington, D.C., area water and wastewater treatment plants and worked with the major water and wastewater industry associations. These include

- the Association of Metropolitan Water Agencies (AMWA),
- the National Association of Water Companies (NAWC),
- the American Water Works Association (AWWA),
- the Water Equipment Manufacturers Association (WEMA), and
- the Association of Metropolitan Sewerage Agencies (AMSA).

On December 18, 1998, the Committee held a field hearing on Y2K preparedness in the water and wastewater industry in Anaheim, California. The City of Anaheim Public Utilities Department hosted this hearing. The witnesses were Dana Minerva, EPA Deputy Assistant Administrator for Water; James Brainerd, Chief Information Officer, Los Angeles Department of Water and Power; James Ellisor, Director of Information Systems, Las Vegas Water District; Patrick Miles, Information Technology Director, Orange County Sanitation District; William Hetland, District Manager, El Dorado Irrigation District; and James Bell, Vice President; Technical Services, Smith and Loveless, Inc., (a leading manufacturer of water and wastewater and pumping equipment). Following the hearing, Senator Bennett toured the City of Anaheim Water Services Lenain Water Filtration Plant.

One of the major topics of discussion during the hearing was the need for water and wastewater companies to obtain assurances from their electric power providers that they will be considered "uninterruptable" or priority customers in the event power supply problems occur. Currently, no legal authority exists to require that power utility companies consider water and wastewater companies as priority customers. Such agreements have customarily been negotiated on a case-by-case basis between power and utility companies.

Mr. Jim Ellisor, Director of Information Systems for the Las Vegas Valley Water District, noted in his testimony that some variability exists in water systems' reliance on electricity, depending on system design. He noted that some systems rely completely on gravity and require little or no electricity for their operation, including some large systems.

During her testimony, EPA Deputy Assistant Administrator Dana Minerva noted that the EPA does not consider reliance on switching to the manual mode of operation as the preferred solution to Y2K problems. Manpower limitations were cited during the testimony as one impediment to a company's ability to easily switch to the manual mode of operation. The possibility of creating some type of "reserve force" that could assist companies in need of additional personnel in the event of the need to default to manual mode was discussed. It was concluded that operation of water and wastewater plants in the manual mode requires skilled and certified operators. Consequently, a pool of unskilled reservists from outside of the water industry would probably not provide an effective solution to the manpower shortage problem.

It should also be noted that each water and wastewater treatment system requires operators to possess a body of knowledge specific to those individual systems. Mr. Bill Hetland, General Manager of the El Dorado Irrigation District, stated that most agencies would have to look to their own internal resources to solve the Y2K problem, that it would be unrealistic to think that a pool of labor would be available to assist in Y2K. He also stated that staffing would become an issue for his agency if manual operations were required for an extended period of time.

Mr. Hetland stressed the importance of providing information to the community about the problem. He also described the progress his agency had made and said such information is vital to community preparedness. He also expressed concern about regulatory compliance and the liability issue.

Deputy Assistant Administrator Minerva testified about EPA's implementation of a new policy aimed at encouraging Y2K testing in the water and wastewater industry. This policy waives penalties if violations occur during Y2K testing, provided specific conditions are met. Deputy Assistant Administrator Minerva further stated that testing and preparation would be taken into account if Y2K-related enforcement violations occur on January 1, 2000, or other "problem dates." According to Ms. Minerva, EPA cannot rule out any enforcement pertaining to Y2K problems; however, it will take efforts to resolve the problem into account.

The new EPA policy is limited to testing-related violations disclosed to EPA by February 1, 2000. The policy is subject to conditions which include the need to design and conduct the tests well in advance of the dates in question and to correct any testing-related violations immediately to ensure the protection of human health and the environment.

The General Accounting Office, at the request of this Committee, is currently preparing a survey of state regulatory agencies with jurisdiction over public water and wastewater utility companies. This survey will determine the extent to which state regulatory agencies are assessing the Y2K readiness of public water and wastewater utilities.

In July 1998, Committee staff surveyed 20 water and 20 wastewater companies regarding their Y2K preparedness. About 25% of those contacted responded to the survey, despite the fact that a confidentiality pledge was made to all survey recipients. The results indicate that of the 11 companies that responded to the survey, slightly over 25% stated that it was unlikely they would be Y2K compliant by January 1, 2000. More than 50% of the respondents had not yet completed the initial assessment phase, and 36% did not have contingency plans in place. Of the 64% that had contingency plans in place, the contingency consisted of either switching to manual operations or utilizing parent company operations. The table at the end of this section displays the results of the Committee's survey.

In July and August 1998, the American Water Works Association (AWWA), the Association of Metropolitan Water Agencies (AMWA), and the National Association of Water Companies conducted a joint survey of their memberships regarding Y2K readiness. Approximately 725 of the 4,000 members of these associations responded to this survey.

- About 81% of the respondents expect to complete their internal Y2K work on time.
- About 89% of the community public water systems serving populations ranging from 100,000 to 1 million people expect to have Y2K compliance work completed on time.
- About 87% of the systems serving between 10,001 and 100,000 people expect to complete their work on time.
- About 76% of the systems serving less than 10,000 people expect to be completed on time.
- Only 26% of the respondents reported having fully assessed the compliance status of vital business partners such as power and telecommunications service providers and vendors upon whom they rely.
- About 83% of the respondents reported that they had not completed their Y2K contingency plans.
- About 39% of the respondents reported that they expect to spend less than $10,000 on their Y2K programs.
- About 26% expect to spend $10,000 to $50,000 on their programs.
- About 80% expect to spend $50,000 to $100,000.

- About 10% expect to spend $100,000 to $1 million.
- About 4% expect to spend over $1 million.

In June 1998, the Association of Metropolitan Sewerage Agencies (AMSA) conducted a survey of its 202 members. AMSA is a coalition of publicly owned wastewater treatment agencies. Its member agencies are responsible for collectively treating and reclaiming over 18 billion gallons of wastewater each day. AMSA received 76 responses to its survey. Results indicated the following:

- The level of automation within each agency averaged 54%. (Not all aspects of each agency's operation are automated, i.e., an agency may utilize automated billing but its operational plant processes may be manually controlled.)

Eighty-eight percent of the respondents reported that they currently utilized some form of Supervisory Control and Data Acquisition System (SCADA) in their operations. It should be noted that while an agency might use SCADA in one aspect of its operation, such as monitoring a remote pumping station, this does not mean that its entire system is automated. These systems are pervasive in the power and water and wastewater utility industries and typically collect and transmit data about flow, pressure, and temperature. Computers can be utilized at any point in the system where measurements are made regarding pressure, water quality, chemical content, treatment, time, or billing.

- Nearly 100% of the respondents reported that they use computers for process control, laboratory research, industrial compliance, billing systems, and other administrative purposes, such as finances, inventory, and maintenance management.

- Ninety percent of the respondents have developed a plan to assess and address the Y2K issue.
- Forty-five percent of the respondents reported estimated Y2K costs ranging from $0 to $100,000. Fifteen percent reported estimated costs in excess of $1 million, with two respondents reporting estimates of $15 million. Most of the agencies reporting costs in excess of $1 million were relatively large systems, but 17% of those reporting costs in excess of $1 million were agencies which served under 250,000 people. Most agencies estimated Y2K costs between 0 and 2 percent of their operating costs.
- Approximately 95% of the respondents reported they had begun to implement Y2K solutions, and 26% reported they were complete or nearly complete in their Y2K preparation.
- Approximately 55% of the respondents reported having a backup plan should all or a portion of their systems fail as a result of Y2K.

Concerns

With very few exceptions, the ability of the water utilities to supply fresh, clean drinking water and to effectively treat wastewater is linked directly to the utilities' ability to obtain a continuous and reliable source of electric power. This fact underscores the importance of the topic of this Committee's hearing on June 12, regarding the Y2K problem and electric power utilities.

While some water and wastewater utilities can generate their own electricity in the event of a power outage, the ability to do so for an extended period of time would depend upon the availability of a steady supply of diesel or other alternative fuel to power the utilities' independent generators. In general, the larger water and wastewater utilities do maintain the ability to generate their own source of back-up electricity, but the duration for which this can be done varies widely within the industry.

There is no interconnectivity built into the water distribution system as with the electric power grid. Nevertheless, some citizens could be facing interruptions of water utility service on January 1, 2000, if water utility companies do not adequately address the Y2K problem.

Water industry Y2K issues are broader and more complex than simply whether electric power will be available to run the pumping stations. For example, wastewater treatment facilities and water supply utilities are interrelated. Upstream contamination caused by a malfunctioning wastewater treatment plant would have a direct impact on a fresh water treatment facility located downstream.

The EPA identified six major areas in water and wastewater treatment facilities where embedded computer chips might be located. These are communications infrastructure, instrumentation, facilities and support, materials tracking, production and process, and process controls. The list included 51 individual devices that potentially could contain embedded chip technology.

Of primary concern in the water and wastewater industry is the vulnerability of sensitive SCADA systems utilized in automated water and wastewater processes.

The degree of automation in water and wastewater systems varies widely throughout the country, depending upon both the age and size of the individual systems. Many older systems are not highly computer dependent.

The Committee is concerned about the inability of some wastewater treatment facilities to properly operate in the event of power outages of even moderate duration. Committee staff reviewed numerous cases in which electrical power interruptions led to the discharge of untreated wastewater or raw sewage into rivers or the ocean. Such discharges currently occur on a sporadic basis throughout the country due to power outages and excessive rainfall.

As is true in all other aspects of the Y2K problem, the water and wastewater industry is also vulnerable to supply chain interruptions. Water treatment plants in particular rely on a regular supply of chlorine and other chemicals that are required in the water treatment process. Long-term interruptions in the means of production or delivery of these items due to other Y2K problems would directly impact the utilities' ability to deliver their services. The stockpiling of some of these chemicals prior to the Year 2000 has been proposed by some as a means of alleviating concerns about supply chain interruptions. However, some of the chemicals used in the industry represent a public health hazard if accidentally discharged into the environment. The risk to public safety would be greatly multiplied if some of these chemicals were stockpiled.

Committee staff has reviewed numerous recent examples of computer-related or computer-induced failures in the water and wastewater industry. While the cases reviewed are not believed to be the result of Y2K induced problems, they clearly illustrate the sensitive and important role which computers play in the water and wastewater services area. Numerous water or wastewater companies could be confronted by similar computer-related failures on January 1, 2000, if proper steps are not taken now to address the Y2K issue.

Numerous representatives of the water and wastewater industry offered assurances to Committee staff that they could switch their operations to the manual mode in the event of a Y2K disruption. In their response to the AMSA survey, most wastewater agencies pointed out that switching to the manual mode would present little if any problems since many automated processes run in parallel with manual instrumentation and control. Switching to the manual mode of operation may represent a viable alternative to computer-controlled processes under ideal conditions and in a controlled environment. However, the conditions that might require transition to a manual mode of operation are likely to be neither controlled nor ideal in the case of Y2K.

Company Type	Date Aware of Y2K Problems	Date Formal Project Started	Is Your Assessment Complete	Percent Systems Mission Critical	Contacted Service Providers/ Vendors	Legal or Liability Concerns	Contingency Plans Complete	Contacted by Regulators	Contacted by Investors	Will You Finish in Time
1 water	1996	1996	80%	50%	Yes	Yes	Yes	Yes	Yes	Yes
2 water	1997	1997	No	90%	No	No	Yes	Yes	Yes	Yes
3 water	1997	1997	Yes	50%	No	Yes	Yes	No	Yes	Yes
4 water	1996	1998	No	unknown	No	Yes	No	Yes	Yes	No
5 water	1996	1998	No	unknown	No	No	No	Yes	Yes	unknown
6 waste water	1995	1996	Yes	0%	No	No	Yes	Yes	No	Yes
7 water/waste	1996	1997	Yes	20%	Yes	No	Yes	No	Yes	Yes
8 water/waste	1996	1997	Yes	100%	Yes	Yes	Yes	No	Yes	Yes
9 water/waste	NR	NR	NR	NR	NR	NR	NR	NR	NR	Yes
10 water/waste	1996	1996	No	unknown	Yes	No	No	Yes	No	Yes
11 water/waste	1996	1996	Yes	90%	Yes	No	Yes	Yes	Yes	No

NOTES:
• MC = mission critical, NR = no reply
• Only 27.5% of all water and wastewater companies responded.
• The 8 companies that reported their costs, project that they will spend over $86 million collectively on Y2K.
• Of the 11 companies who responded, 27% reported they would probably not be Y2K compliant.
• More than 50% of the 11 respondents have not finished their companies' initial assessment of compliance.
• Of the 11 water and wastewater companies, 36% do not have contingency plans in place. The 64% who do intend to either use their parent company's system or operate manually.

Water Utility Sector Survey Conducted by Special Committee Staff

On its face the survey data cited here appear to present a somewhat optimistic picture of the Y2K readiness of the water and wastewater industry. However, attention must be paid to the fact that the response rate for each of these surveys was relatively low, and the status of those agencies that did not respond remains largely unknown.

Analysis of the July 1998 joint AMWA/NAWC/AWWA July 1998 survey of water agencies reveals that 14% of responding companies serving populations over 100,000 people reported that they would not have their Y2K compliance work done on time. The exact impact that this will have on their operations is not clear, as it is unknown whether this includes any of their mission-critical systems. Of the 11 companies who responded to the Committee's survey, over 25% indicated that they did not expect to be Y2K compliant by January 1, 2000.

Healthcare

Overview

Healthcare is the largest single industry in the United States. It is a giant of an industry: 750,000 physicians, 5,200 hospitals, annual expenditures of $1.5 trillion, patient utilization census of 3.8 million daily inpatient visits and 20 million daily outpatient visits, a federal Medicare program treating 38 million seniors at an annual cost of $300 billion. Additionally, Americans consume $90 billion worth of medications and medical supplies per year. But, the most important statistic is that average life expectancy has increased from age 47 in 1900, to age 76 in 1998. Today, 70% of Americans will live to be 65, versus 20% in 1910.

Industry Technical Dependency

The increase in life expectancy is the result of many factors: scientific, economic, public education and a host of others. But an underlying cause is technological improvement in every aspect of healthcare. These medical technologies are susceptible to the Y2K problem in three ways.

1. Software

- *Patient data systems* start with admission of a patient to a hospital and the determination of insurance eligibility. All subsequent medical treatment activities, including the results of all diagnostic tests, are automatically computer recorded. This ensures communication between medical specialties, the carrying out of doctor's orders, and the creation of an audit trail to protect the patient and the caregivers.

> *"Y2K could put the healthcare industry in intensive care."*
>
> Senator Chris Dodd

- *Health claim billing systems* are the principal means of financing the huge cost of healthcare. Consequently, the 4 million daily medicare health claims amounting to over $1 billion are 85%-98% computer generated and processed in an Electronic Data Interchange (EDI) mode between provider and payor.

- *Pharmaceutical research, manufacturing and distribution systems* are the basis for providing the patient with effective medications. These systems electronically link the drug wholesaler to its pharmaceutical supplier and distribution outlets, principally retail pharmacies and hospitals. Finally, national direct mail order prescription services operate as both wholesaler and retailer.

2. Embedded Microprocessors

- *Biomedical devices* are the core of medical technology, used by hundreds of millions of units. These devices occur in every kind of diagnostic test equipment (e.g., blood chemistry analyzers, MRI, X-ray, etc.) and therapy (e.g., radiation) both inpatient and outpatient. Additionally there is a heavy usage (8 to 10 thousand per hospital) of biomedical devices in in-patient hospital care. The healthcare industry currently relies on manufacturers' Y2K compliance data reports to determine whether the device will function appropriately when the date changes. Many device manufacturers have published these reports, indicating Y2K compliance status by model and serial number of each device they sell. But some medical device companies still have not informed FDA of the Y2K risks. Committee Vice Chairman, Senator Chris Dodd, formally published the names of these companies in the Congressional Record on September 23, 1998.

- *Infrastructure operations* use microprocessor controls in hospitals, clinics and medical office buildings controlling heating, ventilation, security and air-conditioning, as well as power and water.
- *Process control and analytical devices* are critical for managing quality control in laboratories, manufacturing flow in factories, and automated order activities in warehouses. Tolerances in most of its product are dependent on microprocessors to achieve them.

3. Electronic Interconnections or Interfaces

These are the most prolific and potentially the most likely cause of Y2K failures. For example, a doctor orders, through the hospital information system, that a patient be given an intravenous feeding. The microprocessor controlling the patient's infusion pump is connected to the same hospital information system. The infusion pump records the patient's ID, the quantity of the intravenous solution, and the date and time of the treatment. The patients could be in jeopardy if the hospital system and the biomedical devices are neither Y2K compatible nor compliant.

- *Business partnerships* are electronically linked throughout the industry. Consequently, a critical part of Y2K remediation is to determine if all the business partners of a healthcare entity are Y2K compliant.

Major Initiatives

The Special Committee on the Year 2000 Technology Problem held two hearings dealing with healthcare issues. The first hearing was on July 23, 1998, "The Year 2000 Computer Problem: Will the Healthcare Industry Be Ready?" The second hearing, dealing with Y2K problems of general business, was held on October 7, 1998. This hearing included a panel dedicated to the pharmaceutical industry with witnesses from a major pharmaceutical company, a large wholesale drug company, the national association representing wholesale druggists, and an independent pharmacy.

Industry Y2K Perspective

The Gartner Group, a survey research company, issued reports stating the healthcare industry lags behind others in dealing with the Y2K problem in managerial attention, technical resources available, financial resources committed and remediation monitoring.

An additional problem is a highly decentralized system is used to process health claim payments, the underpinning of healthcare financing. It is comprised of a government-insurance industry mechanism that electronically processes nearly 4 million Medicare claims worth over $1 billion daily at over 70 separate locations. Third party payors for private health claims utilize a similar type of electronic claims process.

Hearing Summary

The following issues arose during the course of the hearings.

1. Biomedical Devices

These devices are the Trojan horses in the healthcare industry's compliance. Users are often unaware or unknowledgeable about the impact of the microprocessors inside these sophisticated machines. For example, surgical suite machines such as a $40,000 blood gas analyzer could close down operating rooms if they cannot function on January 1, 2000. Every major medical organization testified that they were experiencing significant problems with biomedical device manufacturers. In many cases, manufacturers were unable or unwilling to comment on their product's ability to function after the millennium change.

- After 2 letters of request, only 500 out of 2,700 companies responded to an FDA survey.
- The Committee requested the FDA legal counsel to respond to this issue: Does the FDA have legal authority to require publication of biomedical devices? The FDA responded that it does not have blanket authority to require all device manufacturers to submit Y2K compliance reports. But, the FDA indicated that in the interest of patient safety, manufacturers should inform the FDA of device problems and corrections.
- The Veterans Health Administration sent letters of request to 1,600 firms for information on purchased medical devices. After three mailings, 233 firms failed to respond.
- The Health Industry Manufacturers Association (HIMA) initially said that it preferred for each manufacturer to work with each customer rather than publicly publish Y2K compliance data. But subsequently, HIMA informed the Committee that they encouraged their members to work with the FDA in providing public disclosure of Y2K compliance data.
- The Committee called upon all manufacturers of biomedical devices to publish relevant and accurate Y2K

data for their machines in a central repository, the FDA
Internet web site.

- The Committee requested that the Food and Drug
  Administration publish a list of biomedical manufacturing companies that have not replied to FDA requests for
  Y2K data by July 30, 1998.
- The Committee stated if the biomedical manufacturers
  were unwilling to respond voluntarily to providing data
  that can save patients' lives, the Congress will enact legislation promptly making mandatory the publication of
  such data. In response, device manufacturers began providing compliance data to FDA for publication on their
  Internet website.

2. Rural and Inner City Hospitals

Rural and inner city hospitals have unique Y2K problems. First,
because these types of hospitals tend to have limited financing,
the expensive discovery, renovation, and testing process is
beyond their means. Second, these institutions do not have
access to the highly skilled personnel needed to achieve Y2K
compliance. Third, these hospitals are more likely to have older
medical equipment, which may be disproportionately subject to
Y2K problems.

- The Committee requested direction from the American
  Hospital Association (AHA) on handling the rural-inner
  city hospital Y2K problem. The AHA stated in corre-
  spondence, it did not have adequate data at present to
  know the ultimate cost. AHA stated that a coalition of
  smaller hospitals is being formed to share Y2K information.
- The Committee stated its concern with the American
  Medical Association (AMA), AHA and FDA about the
  need of a contingency plan for all hospitals. Rural and

inner city hospitals in particular need a fall back if Y2K
compliance is incomplete. The associations stated the
Joint Commission on Accreditation of Healthcare Organizations (JCAHO), the hospital licensing body, already
requires disaster and contingency plans be in place.
However, the Committee does not believe JCAHO
requirements adequately anticipated the extent of Y2K
problems. Also JCAHO only reviews hospitals on a trien-
nial basis.

3. Medical Health Claims Payment-Medicare

The 38 million Medicare recipients, 5,200 hospitals and 780,000
physicians depend on 4 million Medicare claims for $1 billion in
daily payment. Any significant failure or delay of Medicare payments would have a disastrous cash flow effect on their employees, suppliers and communities. The Healthcare Financing
Administration (HCFA), the agency responsible for Medicare
disbursements, gave an unsettling report on how they recently
discovered 30 million more lines of code that needed remediation.

- The Committee asked the HCFA Administrator how the
  agency was going to handle a workload that had grown
  by two and one half times since a July 7 briefing to the
  Committee staff. The Administrator responded that the
  remediation would be the most extensive and expensive
  in the history of Medicare-care and HCFA was taking
  extraordinary steps to meet Y2K deadlines.
- The Committee asked the HCFA Administrator the current level of Y2K compliance of the external Medicare
  payment systems maintained by contractors—the core of
  Medicare payments. The most recent data supplied by
  the Office of Management and Budget (OMB) on
  November 13, 1998, demonstrates that HCFA has tested

only 8 out of 108 external systems. However, the HCFA staff, in a late November meeting with the Committee, indicated substantial progress since the OMB report. Medicare renovation was to be completed by December 31, 1998, and full testing in the spring of 1999. None of these systems are Y2K compliant as of February 24, 1999.

- The Blue Cross/Blue Shield (BC/BS) representative assured the Committee that their organization, the largest Medicare contractor, would be ready on time for the December deadline. However, the OMB report referenced above, raises questions of completion dates. The GAO report of February 24, 1999, indicates Y2K problems continue at all BC/BS sites.

- The Committee raised the issue of contingency planning for Medicare payment processing in the event of contractor failure in meeting the Y2K deadlines. The HCFA administrator and BC/BS were requested to tell Congress about specific contingency plans when they are available. At present only general contractor directions for planning are available in lieu of specific plans.

4. The Domino Effect of Y2K Failure

Perhaps the most disturbing Y2K revelation to the Committee was the disclosure of the domino effect of Y2K failure. It can occur in both the use of biomedical devices and in Medicare payments.

- If one biomedical device malfunctions, it can potentially shut down an operating room. Or even worse, one device can pass erroneous data onto other devices creating adverse patient conditions. In other words, Y2K mistakes can reverberate throughout the healthcare system.

- An exhibit displayed at the hearing showed the pathway for Medicare hospital claims, 98% of which are processed electronically. Each claim must pass through a series of steps beginning with patient eligibility at the hospital through final Medicare payments. A Y2K problem at any step in the process, could either delay payment or fail to remit payment.

Assessments

Based on Committee hearings in July and October, subsequent meetings with healthcare industry personnel, and the October 17, 1998, Gartner Group Report, healthcare lags in its progress towards Y2K preparedness. Assessment is broken into the five portions of the industry: pharmaceuticals, large hospitals and hospital chains, health claim billing systems, rural and inner city hospitals, and doctors' offices.

Progress of Healthcare Industry Segments

1. Pharmaceuticals

The Pharmaceutical segment of the industry appears best prepared to meet Y2K challenges. As an industry, pharmaceuticals benefited from an earlier start, their far-sightedness partially due to a long time-to-market horizon for their products. Furthermore, top management recognized Y2K as a business risk and provided the necessary management and resources to address it. This industry is reported to be selectively stockpiling basic medical ingredients that could be in short supply. This assures that the industry will be capable of meeting strict FDA requirements for controlling batch source inputs to all medications. However, pharmaceutical companies face potential problems.

The first problem is the dependency on foreign suppliers and subsidiaries. The drug industry operates manufacturing plants worldwide that supply the U.S. market. Some suppliers exist in countries where basic infrastructures lack Y2K preparedness. A further complication is the high concentration of some drug production in foreign countries. Denmark, for example, produces 70% of the world's supply of insulin. Additionally 80% of the basic ingredients for pharmaceutical products produced in the U.S. come from abroad.

The just-in-time (JIT) inventory process presents another problem. JIT has replaced the large wholesale drug warehouses of the past with much more efficient Electronic Data Interchange (EDI) ordering and billing processes. JIT requires smaller warehouses and saves money. If adequate drug inventories are to be maintained locally, pharmaceutical products must be delivered promptly from a manufacturer to a wholesale drug company, then to retail pharmacists and hospitals. This can only occur if the telecommunication/transportation infrastructure functions.

Finally, pharmaceutical companies have a myriad of business partners, which must be Y2K compliant to be effective. Testing all of these electronic relationships is a challenging assignment for the industry.

2. Large Hospitals

While not as prompt as pharmaceuticals in responding to Y2K, large hospitals are dedicating considerable resources towards fixing the problem. They have all the usual Y2K problems of healthcare plus building management concerns. They have to provide water and power, heating, ventilating and air conditioning, plus maintain elevators and security systems. Hospitals must also address Y2K problems in biomedical devices and patient data systems. All of the above must function in harmony for the patient to be adequately protected. Hospital management is playing a catch up game.

As of October, a Gartner Group Report indicates that 64% of hospitals do not plan to test their Y2K software remediation—a disquieting fact which hearings in 1999 will attempt to verify. Second, many hospitals are relying solely on producers of medical devices to certify their Y2K compliance. Based on known inaccuracies of some producers' compliance certification, this could be a serious mistake. Third, Y2K contingency planning is in its infancy at hospitals.

3. Health Claim Billing Systems

Automated billing is the underpinning of the healthcare system. This $1.5 trillion industry is almost totally dependent on third party payors (insurance companies, Medicare/Medicaid) that finance colossal healthcare expenditures. Progress is moving very slowly.

Medicare (responsible for 40%-50% of all payments), has zero Y2K compliant payment programs, according to the most recent GAO report. Medicaid, the federal-state healthcare payment system, has widely varying stages of Y2K remediation progress that differs from state to state. A General Accounting Office report dated November 6, 1998, indicates that only 17 states have completed the renovation phase. No state has claimed victory in meeting Y2K goals.

The private sector has also experienced difficulties. In a recent publication of Securities Exchange Commission (SEC) 10Q financial reports, one of the largest private insurers recently set aside nearly $200 million to renovate its Y2K healthcare billing systems. This indicates that significantly more Y2K remediation is required.

4. Rural and Inner City Hospitals

Rural and inner city hospitals depend on older equipment much more than large well-endowed hospitals do. On the plus side, low tech equipment may not have any Y2K exposure. On the negative, older versions of bill payment software are more likely to be noncompliant. The concern for rural and inner city hospitals stems from their lack of resources to prepare or test for Y2K problems. Additionally, it is unclear how aware rural and inner city hospitals are of Y2K problems.

5. Doctors' Offices

Because the nation's nearly 800,000 doctors work out of thousands of separate offices, detailed data on the extent of the Y2K problem in this area is unavailable. (Gartner Group Reports are uncertain on the status of this healthcare area.) Offices have all the Y2K problems similar to hospitals on a smaller scale but *without* the comparable access to technical and financial resources. Since diagnostic testing depends upon biomedical devices, potential problems may exist. Patient data systems are not widely used in doctors' offices today, but electronic health claims billing systems are nearly universal for Medicare. If doctors have to return to paper billing because of Y2K failures, insurance companies and Medicare would be hard pressed to accommodate the resulting volume of health claims.

Concerns

There are substantial indications that in some healthcare settings, insufficient attention is being paid to Y2K issues. The October 17, 1998, Gartner Group Report paints a dismal picture of healthcare industry preparation for Y2K. Top management needs to engage this problem as a group, perhaps by formalizing compliance programs through governing bodies or industry groups.

Based on a 1996 National Institutes of Health Report, nearly 40 million Americans are chronically ill or physically impaired. Maintenance of adequate drug inventories can be a life and death matter for patients dependent on drugs for survival, such as insulin for 10 million diabetics. Since some of these life saving drugs have a short shelf life, how will the healthcare system be structured to ensure availability of life dependent medications?

The Committee recognizes that medical malpractice insurance is the means by which both hospitals and medical doctors protect themselves against substantial loss. The insurance industry has already demonstrated an unwillingness to subject itself to Y2K liability. But hospitals and medical practitioners cannot function without liability insurance.

The Committee is also concerned that Y2K prepared hospitals may not follow proper documentation of remediation efforts. Compounding the problem, due diligence standards in this area have not been set.

The healthcare industry is faced with increased costs of Y2K remediation in 1999 and the possibility of extensive litigation after January 2000. How can costs affecting patient care services be controlled?

Excess supplies of non-compliant medical equipment will be available prior to, and after January 2000 due to replacements with compliant systems.

How will patient care be protected when this excess equipment is disposed of either domestically or internationally?

Healthcare managers are currently considering contingency planning programs. What is the optimal use of this approach in protecting patient care considering the multiple risks that can occur in any single facility?

Healthcare systems are trying to reduce Y2K exposure by excluding high-risk business partners from future deals. The cumulative impact of this practice in healthcare and other industries could negatively impact smaller firms irrespective of their competence or cost competitiveness. What can be done to ensure that a "flight to quality" will include Y2K compliant smaller firms?

Rural and inner city hospitals could be endangered as a result of Y2K issues cited above. In many communities they are the center of health activities because of the low-income status of their patients. Furthermore, in rural communities these hospitals are frequently the largest employer. What public policy actions need to be taken promptly before the window of opportunity closes on solutions prior to the Year 2000?

How do the healthcare payment organizations (health insurance companies and Medicare/Medicaid) plan to function if their own payment systems are not working or their customers (hospitals and doctors' offices) cannot produce EDI health claims?

The volume of electronic interfaces (paths) between biomedical devices and patient data and billing systems within hospitals is staggering. How will all the paths be tested adequately for patient safety? What testing standards are being employed to ensure the results will protect patient safety and financial accuracy?

Contingency planning includes disaster recovery plans. Will contingency planners accomplish their work soon enough to be of practical assistance to the continuity of operations for patient safety and proper medical functions?

Several of the national associations that represent the healthcare industry were impressive in their assistance to the Committee and the country. They helped the Committee explain the extent and depth of Y2K compliance issues in their industry. It is obvious from the hearing, however, that no single organization or groupings of healthcare organization, are working together to assure the American public that the major issues are being addressed adequately. Can this industry unify quickly enough to insure that healthcare will become Y2K compliant before the Year 2000?

Testing of renovated biomedical devices, patient data systems and healthcare billing systems is in its early stages. The credibility of the test results is dependent on the quality of the testing criteria and processes. The Committee has not seen any data or discussion dealing with this ultimate measure of Y2K compliance.

Telecommunications

Overview

The telecommunications industry is not immune from the Y2K threat. Y2K-related problems in telecommunications could have serious consequences for both national and economic security. One-third of all electric power controls, the nation's financial transactions and over 90% of defense communications rely on the smooth functioning of public telecommunications. Telecommunications also make possible the remote control of pipelines and transportation systems like air traffic control.

The 99.9% availability of telecommunications in the U.S. can make it easy to forget how much we depend upon this critical infrastructure.[1] However, the failure of AT&T's frame relay system in April 1998 and the loss of PanAmSat's Galaxy IV satellite in May 1998 remind us just how much we take telecommunications for granted. When AT&T's nationwide frame relay system for data transmission crashed, one bank lost over 1,000 ATM sites and a national retailer experienced problems in over 2,300 stores. When Galaxy IV disconnected 40 million people from their pagers, the effect was felt strongly throughout the economy, including healthcare which could not page critical person-nel. While these failures were not Y2K related, some think they are indicative of the types of inconveniences that may result from the millennium rollover.

Our critical dependence upon com-munications certainly suggested an industry wide response. However, fears of competition and liability prevented a formal coordinated industry-wide approach until late in 1998.

The telecommuni-cations industry is not immune from the Y2K threat.

Telecommunications used to mean switched voice communications. How-ever, the synthesis of computers and telecommunications has broadened the way in which we think about telecommunications. The public switched network (PSN) can be defined as any switching system or voice, data, or video transmission system that is used to provide communica-tion services to the public (e.g., public switched networks, pub-lic data networks, private line services, wireless services, wireless systems, and signaling networks).[2] Many layers of hardware and software enable the seamless communications, which allow us to make phone calls, surf the web, and transact business.

The PSN can be divided into three components:

• PSN elements
• support systems (operations, administrative and mainte-nance systems of the service providers)
• customer premise equipment

Public Switched Network Elements

Public switched network elements include many different devices (any one of which can have Y2K problems) that connect calls between networks. Switches, the most common telephone equipment, establish connections between two telephones when a call is made, with multiple switches required for long distance calls. Switches record the starting and ending times of a call, including the day and the year (which is necessary for calls that cross time zones). If some of the switches used in placing a call are Y2K compliant and others are not, or if the renovations are not performed in a consistent way for the different types of switches made by different manufacturers, the systems may not be able to work together.

Getting a basic dial tone at midnight on January 1, 2000, is less likely to be a problem than disruptions in billing.

Support Systems
In testimony before the Committee Dr. Judith List, Vice President-Integrated Technology Solutions at Bellcore, explained that there is little date sensitive information in the fundamental call processing or data routing capabilities of networks. "Where we do see date sensitive information is in the operations, administration, and maintenance functions of networks," she said. Examples of these types of functions include billing, provisioning of services, network surveillance and maintenance, and other network management and administration functions.

The disruption of a carrier's operations, administration, and maintenance functions could cause some confusion for consumers with inaccurate billing and delays in the service requests. There is a concern that a buildup of errors could eventually begin to degrade service.[3]

According to a report from a high level federal advisory committee released September 10, 1998, Y2K problems could impact telecommunications in the following ways:

• *Platform operation (hardware).* Hardware clocks may not recognize the year 2000.

- *Operating system functionality.* Date functions may return the wrong year to applications.
- *Scheduling of events.* Errors in calendar dates can prevent scheduled events (e.g., report updates, testing, designing, provisioning, or billing) from running and can result in incipient failures.
- *Historical data.* Historical data may not be available from 1999, or 1999 may be reordered, with events occurring in 1999 sequenced after 2000.
- *Sorting and searching algorithms.* Dates after 1999 will be ordered before 1999; searching algorithms intended to include dates in 2000 (e.g., "Where date > 1997") will exclude them instead.
- *Password expiration.* All passwords may expire (which would prevent authorized users from performing legitimate functions), or they may never expire (which could diminish the protection offered by password aging).[4]

Customer Premise Equipment

Customer premise equipment (CPE) is also vulnerable to Y2K problems. CPE includes:

- Private branch exchange equipment (PBX)
- telephone equipment
- cellular phones
- fax machines
- private data networks
- public service answering points

Many small and medium sized businesses may not be aware that their privately owned communications equipment may fail because of Y2K problems. If businesses do not take a proactive approach by contacting vendors and obtaining the manufacturer's compliance information, they could have difficulty maintaining normal business functions due to the failure of their own communications equipment. The good news is CPE will not cause disruptions in the public network. However, the economic impact on businesses with failed telecommunications systems may be equally as damaging.

According to the Gartner Group, networking equipment produced before 1996 has only a 50% chance of transitioning to the year 2000 without needing to be upgraded or replaced. Gartner also cautioned that local area networks (LANs) can be impacted by Y2K in a number of different ways including total failure and denying management access.[5] In view of their projection that 20% of the web servers installed prior to 1997 could fail to function properly through January 2000, the Gartner Group also warned disruptions might ultimately deny 5 percent of Internet user connectivity. Gartner is also projecting that 90% of web users could experience delays. In addition, 30% may find sites unreachable.

Competition for resources in January 2000 may make it difficult for small and medium-sized business to secure help. It is imperative that businesses and other organizations make communications a priority now.

Y2K Initiatives in Telecommunications

Numerous Y2K initiatives are currently underway in the telecommunications industry, including strong efforts by the Federal Communications Commission (FCC), the Network Reliability and Interoperability Council (NRIC), the Telco 2000 Forum and Alliance for Telecommunications Industry Solutions (ATIS), the National Communications Systems (NCS), and the President's National Security Telecommunications Advisory Committee (NSTAC).

The FCC

Since 1934, the FCC has regulated interstate and international communications, including radio, television, wire, satellite and cable. In July 1997, the NRIC, the FCC's federal advisory committee, presented its findings and recommendations on the implementation of the Telecommunications Act of 1996 in a report entitled Network Interoperability: The Key to Competition. The report observed that *"interconnectors must ensure that their year 2000 conversion efforts are compatible."*[6] However, NRIC made no specific recommendations for an industry-wide response to the problem.

In the summer of 1997, the Y2K problem was viewed as a due diligence effort, which only needed to be addressed by individual companies. There did not appear to be a role for the FCC or a need for a coordinated industry-wide response to the Y2K problem. The lack of strong national leadership made it very easy to defer the problem. Commissioner Michael Powell was appointed to the FCC in December 1997. In his role as the FCC Defense Commissioner, he began an aggressive Y2K awareness outreach to the industry.

"Despite carriers' best efforts to correct Y2K problems and carrier assurances that telephone service will be available on January 1, 2000, the FCC, most industry analysts, and even some carrier representatives conceded that some failures are still likely to occur."[7] However, the types of problems that could result remain unclear.

In March 1998, Senator Jon Kyl wrote to the Chairman of the FCC and expressed his concern about the absence of an industry-wide telecommunications effort to test for interoperability, or an accurate assessment of the industry of how Y2K may affect the Public Network (PN).[8] Senator Kyl also suggested that if NRIC was tasked by the FCC, it could produce an accurate and much needed assessment of how the Y2K problem could affect the PN. This assessment could look beyond the traditional switched network and consider other communication technologies including cellular and satellite among others. Such a report could well provide the basis for building contingency plans to ensure that communications vital to national and economic security could be maintained.

On April 28, 1998, before the Senate Commerce Committee, FCC Chairman William Kennard testified that the NRIC would be asked to examine the implications of Y2K on communications. On July 30th, a day before presenting testimony to the Y2K Committee, the FCC announced that Michael Armstrong, CEO of AT&T, would chair the newly rechartered federal advisory group to look at Y2K. The NRIC met to propose a comprehensive plan examining three main areas:

- Y2K Impact on the Networks
- Y2K Impact on Customer Premise Equipment
- Network Reliability.

Telco 2000 Forum

One of the earliest and best-organized efforts to test for interoperability in the PN was the Telco Year 2000 Forum. Collectively representing about 145 million access lines, The Forum diligently sought to overcome the complexity of sharing information and antitrust concerns in the highly charged legal atmosphere of 1997 and 1998. The Forum, a voluntary group of eight local exchange carriers, was the first telecommunications initiative to begin identifying possible problems of interoperability. The Forum members include:

- Ameritech Corporation
- Bell Atlantic
- BellSouth
- Cincinnati Bell
- GTE
- SBC

- Southern New England Telecommunications Corporation
- US West

In an effort to reduce the possible risk of network failures, the Forum began testing in July 1998 and completed testing in January 1999. The Forum completed 1,700 tests and found only seven problem areas, five of which have already been remedied. The Forum tested 16 separate configurations of network elements and data transactions and 40 unique network management configurations. These test configurations were made up of 82 commonly used telecommunications products from 21 suppliers. The Forum specifically examined the impact of Y2K fixes and interoperability on:

- Emergency services
- Basic, enhanced, and intelligent services
- Network management systems
- Data networks

The tests were concluded successfully at the end of 1998. A report is expected by the end of January 1999. The early initiative of the Forum and its commitment to business continuity will play a major role in alleviating public concern. According to expert testimony from Gerry Roth of GTE, *"Despite the fact that this network cannot be 100 percent tested in advance of the Year 2000, we believe our individual and collective actions in Year 2000 remediation and subsequent test and validation provide a basis for continued confidence that the telephone and data networks will continue to operate and provide the outstanding services we have come to expect."*[9]

Alliance for Telecommunications Industry Solutions

On January 4, 1999, ATIS began scheduled internetwork interoperability testing to evaluate the impact of the Year 2000 date change on the PSN. Companies participating in the testing include Ameritech, US West, GTE, AT&T and Sprint, as well as six wireless service providers (Aerial Communications, AirTouch, AT&T Wireless, Bell Atlantic Mobile, BellSouth and SBC).

Planning and implementation of the testing procedures began several months ago. Efforts included identification of the test's scope, generation of appropriate test scripts, and obtaining participants to donate lab equipment and the appropriate resources. Interconnected services to be tested on the network include toll free services; Local Number Portability (LNP); the Government Emergency Telecommunications System (GETS); and wireline-to-wireless and wireless-to-wireline interconnections.

All testing is being conducted off-line to ensure no disruption of existing services to the PN. This testing effort will be accomplished by rolling forward the dates of the interconnected switches in a laboratory environment to simulate the following date rollovers:

- December 31, 1999, to January 1, 2000
- February 28 to February 29, 2000
- February 29 to March 1, 2000
- December 31, 2000, to January 1, 2001

During each simulated rollover, the signaling network will be monitored to ensure that the PN responds in a satisfactory manner.

ATIS will be testing the internet-working aspects of the PN. ATIS has designed special test scripts that will focus on time-critical network events on 31 December–1 January to model and monitor potential network congestion and the transmission of voice and data from local exchange to inter-exchange carriers, "800" number access, and network management and control. Year 2000 testing will continue through February 12, with results made publicly available to interested parties on April 14, 1999.

Assessment

During 1998, there were no publicly released comprehensive studies or assessments of how Y2K could affect the telecommunications infrastructure. However, it is generally believed that Y2K will not cause prolonged disruptions. The absence of any comprehensive assessment sparked considerable uneasiness among business sectors and the public in general. The general view was that companies were working hard to address Y2K, but little factual information was available.

On January 14, 1999, NRIC released its preliminary assessments demonstrating that the telecommunications industry was meeting the Y2K challenge. NRIC estimates that the majority of the industry is on target to meet its self-imposed goal of Y2K readiness by June 1999. According to the FCC Advisory Committee, local, exchange carrier, long distance carrier and small telephone companies all seemed to be making good progress. However, small phone companies tend to lag approximately 10-15% behind larger local exchange carriers in fixing Y2K problems. The local exchange companies participating in the NRIC (approximately 99% of all the switched access lines in the U.S.) were projecting to have completed 76% of their Y2K renovations by December 1998. The three major long distance carriers participating in NRIC—AT&T, MCIWorldcom and Sprint—represent 82% of the market revenues. These companies are projected to have reached 81% readiness by December 1998. The NRIC assessment is an important first step.

Rural Telephone Companies

The readiness of the 1,271 small companies, who provide about 1% of the access lines in the U.S., remains unclear. Some people within the rural telephone companies, contrary to popular press, pride themselves on maintaining the latest equipment. Some rural companies, for example, claim to have been the first to offer digital switching. Approximately 75% of the rural market is already scheduled for Y2K upgrades. Only 2% are not expected to be Y2K ready.[10]

Satellite Communications

Ramu Potarazu, Chief Information Officer (CIO), INTELSAT, testified before the Committee that communications satellites do not reference a time and a date; rather, a satellite references what is commonly referred to as "satellite local time," that is a reference to the sun. When there is a technological reference to the sun, there usually is no reference to a specific year. INTELSAT's own analysis found that the primary problems reside in ground systems that fly, command and control, and monitor satellites.[11]

INTELSAT expressed concern about ground station users who have computer systems that may not have been upgraded over the last 10 or 15 years. According to INTELSAT, these users may have a more limited knowledge of computers because they only repair the computer system when it breaks. They may or may not be fully aware of the Y2K issue, and they may or may not be remediating any Y2K issues. The users that have out-dated systems do not have money to remediate any Year 2000 issues and sometimes don't even have the money to recognize that they have a Y2K problem. Many of the earth stations throughout the world have several hundred pieces of computer equipment from various manufacturers that control their ability to receive telecommunications information. For example, if antenna control units fail the antenna could not point to the satellite and no information could be sent or received.

"A significant part of INTELSAT's international communications is a two-way communication that uses an INTELSAT satellite between country A and country B. If country A's ground network is Year 2000 compliant; and INTELSAT, being the supply chain in the middle, is also compliant; and country B's ground

network is not Year 2000 compliant, then you will have a failure of the complete chain."[12]

Cable, Mass Media and Wireless

Not much is known about the state of the cable, mass media or wireless industries. The FCC's Cable Bureau is in the second phase of its survey. The survey was sent to companies accounting for approximately 78% of the market share of cable subscribers. The first survey began in April 1998 and found that while most of the companies surveyed had started assessments, there was little progress in remediation. In November 1998, the Cable Bureau began its second survey that covers about 90% of all cable subscribers. Response should be back and assessed some time in the first quarter of 1999. It is also expected that the Mass Media and Wireless Bureaus will have completed initial assessments by the first quarter of 1999.

Concerns

The Committee has three outstanding concerns in communications:

- increased contingency planning among carriers
- increased attention to Y2K security concerns
- international communications

Contingency Planning

Carriers have undertaken massive code corrections, which will be in place by the end of 1998. The large number of code corrections increase the possibility of disruptions from the introduction of new errors.[13] In testimony before the Committee, Judith List, Ph.D., vice president and general manager, Integrated Technology Solutions Business Unit, Bellcore, noted the following:

Finally, there will be problems, and there is a level of uncertainty in this area that makes it difficult to predict where the problems will be. In the software industry today, the best in class companies find 95 percent of code anomalies before the software ever gets to the field. That means that 5 percent of software anomalies are found after the code is operational. Furthermore, according to the Software Engineering Institute, a new defect is introduced with every approximately 4 1/2 fixes of software code. Both of these statistics suggest that, given the pervasiveness and extent of Year 2000 elements, there will be problems. Furthermore, Y2K contingency planning and disaster recovery needs to address plans differently than traditional business continuity plans because backup systems are likely to have the same Year 2000 problems, issues may be more widespread across a number of industries, and problems may last for a longer period of time.

In October 1997, the President's Commission on Critical Infrastructure Protection expressed concerns: *"The unbundling of local networks mandated by the Telecommunications Act of 1996 has the potential to create millions of new interconnections without any significant increase in the size or redundancy of network plants. Unbundling will be implemented at a time of rapid and large-scale change in network technologies. The interaction of complexity and new technologies will almost certainly expand the universe of ways in which system failure can occur, and, unlike natural disasters, there is no assurance that such failures will be localized."*[14]

Telecommunications in the U.S. has one of the most highly developed systems of infrastructure assurance. In 1963, the NCS was created to ensure the federal government has enduring communications. Composed of 23 federal agencies, the NCS works closely with the telecommunications industry and maintains a coordinating center to resolve failures in the networks that could impact national security or emergency preparedness.

The NCS works closely with the National Security Telecommunications Advisory Committee (NSTAC), an advisory committee created in anticipation of the AT&T divestiture. Composed of 30 chief executive officers from telecommunications, information technology, aerospace and banking companies, the NSTAC makes recommendations to the President on issues critical to protecting the U.S. communications infrastructure. In September 1998, the NSTAC released the first report that examined the impact of Y2K on the assurance of national security and emergency preparedness communications. The NSTAC report noted that *"no organization, either private or government could offer a guarantee of total Y2K problem eradication from its networks, services, or systems. Additionally, these organizations could not offer guarantees of the adequacy of Y2K internetwork interoperability testing."*[15]

In July 1998 the NSTAC testified about the findings of its widespread outage report and highlighted the fact that the industry has had limited experience with systemic, widespread network failures. Both the NCS and the NSTAC believe that the probability for Y2K-related widespread outages is extremely low. However, because of our reliance on communications the cost would be extraordinarily high for commerce and defense. In testimony before the Committee, NSTAC expressed concern about the lack of an industry-wide plan to facilitate intercarrier coordination for recovering from a widespread outage of this nature. Most carriers have internal plans and processes for maintaining the integrity of their own networks. Looking further at contingency planning and recovery from a widespread outage, the NSTAC questioned whether existing communication and coordination mechanisms among service providers were adequate for efficient reconstitution of service. It was unclear whether the existing agreements, communications systems, and coordinating mechanisms in the industry could mitigate a severe widespread service outage.

During reconstitution, a means of communication and coordination between and among critical centers would be indispensable. The NCS works closely with the industry and is uniquely positioned to collect network outage information for Y2K disruptions.[16]

As part of its normal contingency efforts, the NCS maintains a private communications network, which is independent from the PN and provides connectivity to the FCC, all of the regional Bell operating companies, GTE, Sprint, and switch manufacturers. In preparing for Y2K and other threats to the communications infrastructure, the NCS is considering expanding its network to include the Critical Infrastructure Assurance Office, and the National Infrastructure Protection Center. The private network could facilitate reconstitution efforts in the event of serious disruptions. As an additional backup, the NCS maintains high frequency (HF) radio communications with major telecommunications providers and can also access over 1,000 HF radio sites around the world.

Chairman Bennett remained concerned that the administration was not developing the necessary policy to respond to an unanticipated Y2K disruption in the U.S communications infrastructure. In August 1998, Senator Bennett wrote to the Director of the Office of Science and Technology Policy (OSTP), and asked what role the Joint Telecommunications Resources Board (JTRB)[17] would play in the event of a Y2K-related emergency. The Assignment of National Security Emergency Preparedness Telecommunications (Executive Order 12472), tasked the Director of OSTP to maintain a JTRB to advise the President on the emergency allocation of telecommunications resources. The JTRB met in January 1999 for the first time in several years to determine how it might respond to a serious Y2K related event in communications.

Security

The Committee has repeatedly expressed concern about the number of code corrections that are taking place in foreign countries and the long-term security risks that this could cause for information assurance in the U.S. In response to Committee questions about the threat of malicious code, Dr. List responded: *"There is the possibility that security risks can be introduced into any code that is being remediated, not just code that is corrected in foreign countries. Programmers can, for example, introduce trap doors or back doors for non-malicious reasons, for example, to make it easier for them to maintain the code. These trap doors or back doors can then be used for other purposes to obtain unauthorized access to the software program. In other instances, security problems can be introduced for directly malicious purposes during the code remediation process. To date, I know of no easy way to assess code to ascertain the existence of these types of security risks. It requires labor intensive examination of the code, line by line. Companies can work to protect themselves from such risks by conducting adequate due diligence of employees, contractors, and service providers that they may hire to remediate Y2K problems. In addition, implementing various policies (such as code inspections) to monitor the code remediation process also can help reduce risk."*[18]

International Communications

Today global telecommunications is a growing $800 billion industry. Industry analysts note that 75% of all traffic originates or terminates in one of six countries: France, Germany, Italy, Japan, U.K. and the U.S. In addition, 90% of all call traffic comes from 20 countries. Forty percent of the global traffic touches the U.S., 20% Europe, and 15% through Asian hubs.[19] Telecommunications revenues in the U.S. are about $300 billion a year, with the majority of revenues coming from the provision of services.

At the United Nations' "National Y2K Coordinators Meeting" on December 11, 1998, the International Telecommunication Union's (ITU) Year 2000 Task Force outlined global efforts to ensure Y2K readiness in telecommunications.

The ITU established a Y2K task force in March 1998 to raise

the awareness of operators and carriers by providing information on potential Y2K problems. The ITU considers one of the greatest obstacles to global readiness is the lack of awareness and action at the governmental level to pressure telecommunications operators to share information about their Y2K readiness. Part of the ITU's effort has been to recommend compliance standards and also promote the sharing of information. In addition, the ITU has encouraged the sharing of Y2K readiness information with customers. The ITU has had three main goals:

- promote Y2K best practices
- facilitate global interoperability testing
- provide specific guidance on business continuity planning.

The ITU's global assessment is somewhat sketchy at this point. However, according to the ITU, the U.S., Japan, China, Germany, France and the U.K. account for 53% of wireline infrastructure, and all are reported to have Y2K programs in place. The ITU task force also pointed out that 20 territories accounted for 80% of the world's wire-lines, but there were still no details from Italy, Taiwan (Republic of China) or Ukraine. Throughout the first quarter of 1999, the ITU will organize workshops as needed in specific locations including Russia, India and Asia, to promote awareness and to increase knowledge of Y2K readiness.

Some initial testing in September 1998 did not uncover any specific Y2K problems. However, the lack of information about the readiness of global communications remains a serious concern. U.S. carriers are concerned that if foreign companies are not prepared, call completion could be impacted.

Transportation

Overview

The transportation sector is a complex and diverse mixture of public and private enterprises. This sector includes three divisions: aviation, surface transportation and maritime entities. Within each division, distinct "modes" exist. For example, railroads and trucking are both surface modes, but are separate industries in their own right. To keep the scope of the Committee's investigation manageable, the Committee selected areas having a major impact on public safety or the nation's economy. Y2K problems may also exist in areas not covered in this investigation.

Transportation and Y2K Issues

In pursuing this investigation, the Committee staff conducted interviews with a wide variety of knowledgeable parties including: federal agencies that regulate and provide services to transportation system operators, system operators themselves, associations representing a broad cross-section of the industry, equipment manufacturers and facility operators (e.g., airports and ports). A complete list of organizations interviewed is appended to this section.

Like most other sectors of the economy, transportation has become highly automated and dependent on information technology to transport people and goods safely, quickly, and economically. However, such automation has made this sector vulnerable to Y2K concerns and issues seen in other sectors by the Committee. These include obtaining assurance of Government services such as air-traffic control and customs processing, wide variations in individual firms' Y2K preparedness, a profusion of rumors and misinformation, and a general uncertainty about the risk presented by embedded microchips. In addition, the transportation sector raises many concerns about international Y2K preparations. These included the Y2K readiness of international air traffic control, non-U.S. airports, and non-U.S. ports, all of which affect U.S. travelers, businesses, and consumers.

> *"Year 2000 malfunctions in transportation are at their best an inconvenience, but they must not and cannot put our citizens at risk."*
>
> *Senator Chris Dodd, September 1998*

The Committee has found that all the major transportation players—the biggest operators, the largest facilities, the federal agencies, etc.—have substantial Y2K programs underway. In all these programs, the emphasis is first on safety. All of these entities are well on the way to being "Y2K ready" on their own. In addition, parties show a willingness to cooperate with each other in transportation: large airports have reached out to smaller feeder airports and railroads have shared information about Y2K problems. However, there is reason to be concerned about the readiness of smaller players in this sector, as has been the case in other sectors. For example, there are thousands of city and county governments in the U.S. that are responsible for operating and maintaining the local surface transportation infrastructure. The Y2K planning of these governmental entities has been very slow. A good example is highlighted by the September 1998 survey from the comptroller of the state of New York, who found that a disturbingly large number of cities, towns and villages in that state had not, at that time, made any assessment or planning for the Y2K problem.

Major Initiatives

GAO Airport Survey

Airports are a critical component of U.S. aviation operations, often referred to as the National Airspace System (NAS). Airports are the entry and exit points to the NAS for most travelers. While much attention has been centered on the Federal Aviation Administration's ability to guarantee that its air traffic control system will continue to operate safely and efficiently during and after the millennium date change, less attention has been focused on the readiness of the nation's airports.

The Senate Committee on Commerce, Science and Transportation has requested the U.S. General Accounting Office (GAO) to review the Y2K status of the systems and equipment integral to the operation of the nation's airports. At issue are systems for lighting runways, controlling access to secured areas, handling baggage and fueling aircraft.

Highlights of

U.S. Aviation

13 major U.S. airlines

34 national airlines

52 regional airlines

670 certified airports

550 million annual

U.S. passengers

$100 billion total

operating revenues

Breakdowns in these vital systems could disrupt an airport's ability to move aircraft and travelers efficiently and safely and could ripple throughout the entire NAS, thus creating system gridlock.

As part of its review, GAO is surveying more than 400 of the nation's airports to determine progress made toward ensuring that operations will not be seriously affected by Y2K malfunctions. The specific research questions guiding this review are:

- How will the safety, security and efficiency of the NAS be affected if the airports' Y2K preparations are not adequate?
- What conditions will affect the outcome of airports' Y2K preparations?
- What progress have airports made to ensure that their computers and electronic equipment will function on and after January 1, 2000?

The survey data will be supplemented with site visits to a cross-section of airports in order to gather more in-depth knowledge of the challenges faced by airport managers. The report is expected to be available in February 1999.

IATA Survey
The International Air Transport Association (IATA) is the major body for coordinating interairline cooperation. It currently has 260 member airlines from over 130 nations. IATA has been working with its members since 1996 to cope with the millennium bug. IATA members are spending over $1.6 billion to resolve Y2K problems internally.

In 1997, IATA released a survey of 44 of its member airlines on their Y2K preparations and concerns. This survey revealed that 61% of the airlines participating in the survey rated the Y2K problem critical to the industry and another 32% rated it fairly serious. IATA's next initiative has focused on airports around the world. IATA has targeted 100% of the international airports and Air Traffic System (ATS) providers outside of North America and used by IATA members. Although IATA is keeping its survey results private to its member companies, and the public will not be privy to its survey results, the comprehensiveness of IATA's membership should provide reasonable assurance that an airline will not be flying unknowingly into a non-compliant airport in January 2000.

The International Civil Aviation Organization (ICAO) was established in 1947 *"in order that international civil aviation may be developed in a safe and orderly manner and that international air transport services may be established on the basis of equality of opportunity and operated soundly and economically."* In the same year, ICAO became a specialized agency of the United Nations. ICAO now encompasses 185 nations. In an effort to ensure that worldwide air traffic control and international airport operators are fully aware of the scope of the Y2K problem, ICAO has developed an action plan that it is currently implementing. To date, three ICAO "state letters" (advisory letters to member countries) have been distributed: the first on December 1997, the second in May 1998 and the last in November 1998. This is part of an ongoing effort to alert ICAO contracting states to the extent of the problem, to inform them of action being taken by ICAO and to request additional information. While ICAO has no regulatory authority over its member states, it does serve as an adviser to the air-traveling public. In this capacity, ICAO had said that it would publish "status reports on the progress among States in order to provide confidence to the travelling public

Railroad Highlights

Over 700 U.S. railroads

Over 220,000 miles

of track

20,000 locomotives

$32.7 billion in

operating revenue

Over 265,000

employees

20 million intercity

passengers

48 million commuter

passengers

ICAO Status Tracking

and aircraft operators." However, ICAO has at this time dropped its plans to publish these assessment reports.

Assessments

Transportation Sector Survey Conducted by Committee Staff

In preparation for the September 10, 1998 hearing on transportation-related Y2K issues, the staff of the Special Committee on the Year 2000 Technology Problem conducted a survey of large companies and service providers in the transportation sector. The results of this survey are summarized in a table attached to this section.

To sample the transportation sector, representatives were selected from major airlines, airports, railroads, maritime shippers, trucking companies and metropolitan transit authorities. The Committee staff asked survey respondents for information on their automated systems used to manage and operate their respective transportation systems. This included both their computer systems (often referred to as Information Technology or IT) and embedded systems, such as controllers integrated into transportation vehicles or facility control and monitoring systems. In order to facilitate honest and candid answers to survey questions, respondents were given a pledge of confidentiality. Significant items learned from the survey include:

- 62% of the respondents reported that they had not completed their Y2K assessment process. This is disturbing given the short time remaining until December 31, 1999. By comparison, the Office of Management and Budget directed all Federal agencies to complete their assessments by June 1997.
- Six of the eight who answered a question on mission critical systems reported that 70% or more of their systems are mission critical.
- 100% of the respondents reported that their contingency plans are incomplete. Even more disturbing, over half reported that they were not even working on contingency plans at this time.
- 94% reported their total expected Y2K expenditures. The total projected cumulative costs at this time are over $650 million.
- 50% of the respondents reported they anticipated being involved in litigation due to the Y2K problem.
- 94% report they will finish their Y2K preparations on time. The Committee staff feels this is overly optimistic given that most of them have not yet completed the process of fully assessing the scope of their Y2K problem.

Other studies have concluded that medium and small enterprises are not as advanced in their Y2K preparedness as their larger counterparts. Hence, since this study focused on large transportation firms, the results presented here probably represent the best-prepared portion of the industry.

The survey raises many concerns about aviation given the disproportionally poor response rate to the survey of both airports and airlines. Given the concern that already exists about the readiness of the Air Traffic Control system, this will add to the general unease about air travel. The Committee staff finds the case for the Y2K flight readiness of commercial jetliners convincing. Planes will not literally "drop out of the sky" on

January 1, 2000. But, if the ground-based information systems supporting overall air travel are not Y2K compliant, the system will be severely limited in its overall capacity, leading to lost revenue for the airlines, lost productivity in the economy and significant public dissatisfaction with the air transportation system.

Public Transit

Highlights

6,000 U.S. transit

agencies

$7 billion in annual

capital expenses

$19 billion in annual

operating expenses

8 billion trips annually

3.7 billion miles and

246 million hours of

annual service

300,000 employees

The transportation firms surveyed did not become aware of Y2K problems until 1995 or later. Almost all have reported establishing a formal Y2K office and/or project within their company.

Companies are making the best progress on their mainframe and client-server applications and are furthest behind on the embedded chip assessment and remediation aspects of the problem.

Costs varied widely across survey responses. In an attempt to explain this disparity, the Committee found a marked lack of uniform accounting for Y2K expenditures.

A little more than half the surveyed parties were worried about becoming party to litigation brought by Y2K failures or upsets. Still more had concerns about the potential for business partners to fail to deliver expected products or services. Others felt that they could plan for these contingencies.

Organizations were also asked what Congress could do to facilitate Y2K efforts in the transportation sector.

By far, the most common answer (from about 50% of respondents), was to produce legislation that supports good faith sharing of Y2K information and limits the liability organizations are exposed to by Y2K problems, upsets, or failures. Several other actions were mentioned by more than one respondent: (1) Congress should lead in the discovery and dissemination of valid Y2K information to offset the misinformation widely disseminated today, (2) antitrust protection is needed for companies who normally are competitors but who cooperate on Y2K programs and (3) Congress should continually oversee the Y2K programs of federal agencies and service providers important to all industries, such as power utilities and telecommunications.

ATA Survey

The Air Transportation Association (ATA) is the sole trade organization of the U.S. major airlines. The 28 members include all the large U.S. passenger and cargo airlines as well as associate members from Canada, Mexico and Holland. ATA members collectively transport over 95% of all air passengers and cargo in the U.S.

After concern was raised about airports by early surveys and the airlines, ATA has focused an initiative on domestic airports. To date, it has completed 158 awareness and assessment visits in coordination with the Airports Council International and the FAA. In addition, Y2K planning kits have been sent to over 400 airports that the ATA team could not visit.

Testing for Y2K readiness is either underway or soon to begin with the Dallas-Fort Worth Airport, the Seattle-Tacoma Airport and United Airlines. Results of ATA activity and testing were not

Maritime Highlights

The port industry, port users, and capital expenditures for maritime equipment provides:

16 million jobs nationwide

$154 billion in federal taxes

$783 billion of GDP

70% of U.S. Customs revenues

available at the time of this report, but a major readiness announcement is expected from the FAA, ATA and several airlines in the early part of 1999.

Two major issues have been raised in the airport assessments. The first is that airports are often bound by many cumbersome rules when acquiring equipment or services. These rules can be loosened during emergencies and the Committee feels that the FAA, the airports and governing authorities should begin looking at Y2K as an emergency and expedite airport remediation procurements. The second issue is the disparate nature of airport oversight and funding. This unfortunately means that no one general program will work for all airports and Y2K programs will have to be tailored to the specifics of an individual airport.

Concerns

General Concerns

Several general concerns were raised by parties interviewed for this sector including domestic and foreign partner readiness, and federal government readiness. Examples of the first category include airline concerns about airports and airport concerns about jet fuel pipelines. In the second case, the most common concerns were about the Y2K readiness of the FAA's Air Traffic Control systems and U.S. Customs Service's automated import and export systems. The Committee staff met with the General Accounting Office and the Department of Transportation Inspector General on the FAA's Y2K progress and came away with the general sense that the FAA is making substantial progress but still has significant challenges ahead. The Committee also interviewed the U.S. Customs Service on its Y2K preparations. The material presented showed that they were making very good progress in bringing into compliance its "Automated Commercial System," which clears and tracks imports and exports, Y2K compliant.

Aviation-Specific Y2K Issues

Aviation is by far the most complex and automated transportation sector. In the words of one interviewee, "Airlines and airports along with FAA and air traffic service providers rely heavily on Y2K infested technology" and "If today were January 1, 2000, the world's airline system would fail." The major airlines interviewed have substantial Y2K programs and seem to be making significant progress with domestic air operational readiness. However, they expressed concerns about FAA Y2K readiness. Although the airlines stated that the FAA is moving much more deliberately now than a year ago, the airlines are concerned that the FAA still has a long way to go. One airline, which reported doing an independent assessment, said it was satisfied with the validity of the recent FAA announcement that the very important "HOST" computer for the enroute air traffic control centers was not Y2K vulnerable.

However, GAO testified before Congress as recently as August 6, 1998, that the FAA will not be fully ready by January 1, 2000. Significant risks in the FAA remediation program cited by the GAO included:

- Ineffective management of external data exchange analysis and remediation efforts. As of August 6, 1998, half the exchanges were still not examined for date sensitive data; of the 25% found to have date sensitive data, over 90% of those needed repairs.
- Poor coordination to date on international air transportation issues.
- Reliance on a telecommunications infrastructure that is not totally within its control and may not be renovated on time.
- Missteps in business continuity and contingency planning. The National Air Traffic Controller's Association (NATCA) has criticized the current version of FAA's plans for being ambiguous in responding to outages of

critical facilities. The FAA testified at the August 6, 1998, hearing that finalized contingency plans would be available by August 31, 1998, but that date slipped at first until September 30 and then slipped again. At the time of this report, only a draft version of the FAA's Y2K contingency plan is believed to exist and it has not been widely distributed in the aviation community or seen by the Senate Committee.

Airlines can be affected by Y2K in a number of ways other than the loss of Air Traffic Control (ATC). They are heavily dependent on scheduling programs for aircraft, crews and reservations. The aircraft themselves must be flight ready. Airport facilities under their control must be compliant. Moreover, external utilities (e.g., electric power, telecommunications and aviation fuel) must be available. However, the major airlines interviewed by the Committee appear to be managing their internal Y2K preparations well and are surveying their external providers (e.g., foreign airports) for the purpose of developing contingency and business continuity plans.

Airports have many dependencies on information technology that may be Y2K vulnerable. Areas that must be assessed include runway lighting systems and jetway security systems. One airport official has claimed that only one pipeline, originating in Houston, Texas, supplies aviation fuel to most of the airports on the eastern seaboard. If this pipeline were to fail on January 1, 2000, the airports in New York could only operate for four to seven days with the fuel supply on hand. Two surveys are underway on airport readiness: the ATA is surveying domestic airports and the IATA is covering airports abroad. Preliminary information from the ongoing ATA survey indicates that 38% of the 63 airports surveyed do not have a Y2K plan. In addition, concerned U.S. airlines are individually raising Y2K awareness on their initiative because of the late start that IATA had in its efforts.

Concerning aircraft, the Committee interviewed the Boeing Commercial Aircraft Group (BCAG) that provides the preponderance of planes to U.S. carriers. Boeing has done a thorough analysis of all makes and models of Boeing aircraft and aircraft from the recently acquired McDonnell Douglas Corporation (maker of models such as the DC-9s and MD-11s). BCAG contends that a few minor "nuisance" vulnerabilities have been detected in Flight Management Systems on older aircraft. However, the most recent models are all Y2K ready. Boeing has issued service bulletins and service letters on these nuisance factors. Hardware and/or software upgrades are available. In addition, BCAG maintains that these problems will in no way impact the air-worthiness of the aircraft. The Committee staff received the same information from an independent and credible source during a subsequent interview with a major U.S. carrier.

Y2K Issues in Other Transportation Areas

Railroads

Railroads (long haul and short haul) appear to have fewer Y2K transportation equipment problems. As with other large businesses, major internal business systems have to be analyzed and fixed. Concerning operational safety, the short haul railroads have little automation and believe they will not be affected by the century date change. The major railroads interviewed have ongoing Y2K programs and are fixing problems. The most commonly cited operational problem is in train dispatching software, but the Committee staff was informed that even if all of this software were not repaired, the outcome would pose a capacity problem, but not a safety concern.

In earlier testimony before the Senate Banking Committee, it was reported that virtually none of the existing railroad switches are manually switchable. The witness contended that the railroad switches are fully automated and controlled by embedded chips, which are likely to pose substantial Y2K problems. The threat this could pose to economic stability in the U.S. is disconcerting. However, it is the propose of this report to identify and debunk myths like that of the automated railroad switches with embedded chips. As the Committee has learned, concerns about automated railroad switches and signaling systems appear to be ill founded. The Committee staff heard from multiple sources that essentially all automated switches have manual overrides (no source could identify one which didn't). Concerning signaling and warning systems, there didn't appear to be any date-dependent functions that would interfere with their safe operations. These devices are event driven, not date or time dependent. Even in the unlikely event of a Y2K-related failure in this equipment (e.g., a power outage), work-around procedures are in place for continued safe operation of the railroad, although with diminished capacity.

Maritime Transportation

Y2K awareness within the maritime community is low to moderate. Maritime cargo shipping (containerized, bulk, tanker, etc.) is somewhat unique from other transportation modes in that each ship is virtually custom built. Thus, each must be individually inventoried and assessed for Y2K problems. Maritime shipping operational safety is at greatest risk during entry and exit from ports. To avoid increasing that risk due to possible Y2K problems, the concept of keeping ships from entering and exiting ports during the change of century is being considered by shipping operators. If Y2K prevents ports from operating for a lengthy period, there will be a high economic cost to U.S. companies. However, given that the millennium change will occur on New Year's Eve, a short "stand down" period will have minimal economic impact. Due to the long life cycle of ships, major maritime shipping companies' ship inventories often include a variety of ages and automation among ships.

Committee investigation into concerns about the automation of oil tankers did not yield any major Y2K-related safety or environmental issues. There is a large amount of embedded chip technology in material handling equipment at ports. However, assessments of that equipment is still incomplete and it is too early to identify significant issues. Along with revenue systems, cargo tracking, maintenance and scheduling systems are a major concern, since most use commercial, off-the-shelf (COTS) software. Finally, interviewees did not have an accurate sense of the status of international ports. However, it is widely believed that they are far behind in their Y2K efforts. While Y2K impacts on the maritime industry may potentially interrupt commerce, safety is less an issue than in some other industries.

Trucking

There are over 400,000 trucking companies registered with department of motor vehicle agencies in the United States. Eighty percent of these employ fewer than 20 trucks within their operations. The American Trucking Association represents approximately 45,000 individual trucking companies. The trucking industry has become increasingly more reliant on information technology and electronic data interchange in the everyday conduct of business transactions. The process of just-in-time inventory management has drastically reduced reliance on long-term warehouse storage. Consequently, trucking companies have in a sense become mobile warehouses that rely on a dependable stream of up-to-date information in order to effectively service customers.

The trucking industry has become highly time sensitive and uses a sophisticated level of computer software to manage its workload. The load management systems of these companies involve the transfer of electronic data between shippers, brokers, merchants and the trucking companies. This includes transmission of shipping status notices, bills of lading and payment forms. Industry automation extends to advanced onboard vehicle systems that enable a company to remotely monitor a truck's engine performance and speed, and global positioning systems that track a truck's location. Computer technology is also used in advanced weigh-in-motion devices, inspection systems and safety record databases.

Public Transit

In the Public Transit area, the Committee staff interviewed the Washington, D.C., and New York Metropolitan Transit Authorities and the American Public Transit Association (APTA). The Washington MTA program started late and is only in its initial phases. The New York program started much earlier. New York's size creates a challenge, but it also benefits from a much less automated and therefore less Y2K vulnerable system. Finally, APTA has surveyed about 364 of its members. The response rate was about 50%. To quote from the report:

> ... further examination of the data reveals conflicting responses. This raises concern about the ability of transit systems in dealing with Year 2000 issues and their under estimation of Year 2000 problems.

Conclusions

The transportation sector is the lifeblood of our modern economy. Daily, it provides millions of Americans and American businesses with safe, rapid and economical transport of their people and goods. It has been working so well and efficiently that it has turned boats, trucks, trains and even planes into mobile warehouses that efficiently deliver goods to factories and customers on a just-in-time basis.

Segments of the transportation sector work hand in hand as goods and people transfer from one mode to another. This coupling of modes allows the best mode to be used at any given time, but it creates a dependency linkage that leaves the whole

system vulnerable if just one link goes down. Thus it is important that all major segments of transportation be Y2K ready at
the same time if the sector is going to maintain its productivity
after January 1, 2000.

The most disturbing findings in this sector that the Committee has found are:

- Domestic airports have (on average) started very late to
  get ready for Y2K.
- The FAA, although it has made great strides in the past
  year, has a long way to go to be ready for Y2K and
  remains a high risk.
- The situation with international air traffic control and
  airports is much worse than in the U.S. and some level of
  flight rationing is highly possible for some foreign desti-
  nations.
- The maritime shipping industry has not moved aggressively on Y2K. Disruptions to global trade are highly
  likely.
- Public transit systems may not be taking the Y2K problem seriously enough to be ready for the Year 2000.

Transportation Sector Interviews

Transportation Sector Overall
 Department of Transportation (DOT)
 Inspector General's Office
 U.S. Customs Service (Treasury)
 MITRE Corporation

Aviation in General
 General Accounting Office
 Federal Aviation Administration (DOT)
 IBM

Airport Representatives
American Ass'n of Airport Executives
Seattle-Tacoma Airport Authority
Dallas-Fort Worth Airport Authority
New York-New Jersey Port Authority
Airports Council International

Airlines Representatives
Air Transport Association (ATA)
International Air Transport Association
American Airlines
SABRE Technology Solutions
United Airlines
Delta Airlines

Aviation Manufacturers
Boeing Commercial Aircraft

Railroads
Federal Railroad Administration (DOT)
Association of American Railroads
American Shortline Railroad Association
CSX
Amtrak
Burlington Northern-Santa Fe

Shipping
Maritime Administration (DOT)
U.S. Coast Guard (DOT)
American Association of Port Authorities Officials
Crowley Maritime
Sea Land (CSX)
Chevron New
York/New Jersey Port Authority

Company Type	Date Aware of Y2K Problems	Date Formal Project Started	Is Your Assessment Complete	Percent Systems Mission Critical	Contacted Service Providers/ Vendors	*Legal or Liability Concerns	Contingency Plans Complete	Contacts by Creditors	Contacts by Investors	Will You Finish in Time
1 Airline	1995	1995	N	NR	Y	Y	N	Y	Y	Y
2 Airline	1995	1995	N	75% IT 38% emb	Y	Y	N	Y	Y	Y
3 Airline	1995	1996	Y	30%	Y	N	N	Y	Y	Y
4 Airline	1996	1996	N	70%	Y	Y	N	N	N	Y
5 Railroad	1995	1995	N	NR	Y	Y	N	Y	Y	MC only
6 Railroad	1996	1997	N	NR	Y	N	N	Y	N	Y
7 Railroad	early 90's	NR	Y	NR	Y	N	N	Y	Y	Y
8 Railroad	1994	1995	Y	NR	Y	Y	N	Y	N	Y
9 Shipping	1995	1996	Y	100% IT 7% emb.	Y	Y	N	Y	N	Y
10 Shipping	1996	1996	Y	85%	Y	Y	N	N	N	Y
11 Transit Authority	1995	1995	N	75%	Y	Y	N	Y	Y	Y
12 Trucking	1995	1995	70%	Unknown	Y	N	N	Y	Y	Y
13 Trucking	1995	1995	N	NR	Y	Y	N	NR	N	Y
14 Trucking	1995	1995	Y	NR	Y	Y	N	Y	N	Y
15 Trucking	1994	NR	N	75%	Y	N	N	N	N	Y
16 Trucking	1996	NR	N	30%	Y	N	N	N	N	Y

Notes:

*Respondents were asked about potential Y2K legal exposure caused by vendor/supplier failure. Some respondents chose to answer more generally about their overall legal exposure.

•MC = Mission Critical, NR = No Reply, IT = Information Technology (systems), emb. = Embedded (systems)

•For the 15 companies that reported their costs, they project to spend over $650 collectively on Y2K.

Transportation Sector Survey Conducted by Year 2000 Special Committee Staff

Trucking & Highways
Intelligent Transportation Society
American Trucking Association
American Association of State Highway and Transportation
Officials
Federal Highway Administration (DOT)
New York/New Jersey Port Authority
Schneider National

Mass Transit Agencies
Washington MTA
American Public Transit Association
New York MTA

Financial Services

Overview

Both the Subcommittee on Financial Services and Technology and the Special Committee on the Year 2000 Technology Problem examined the financial services sector during the 105th Congress. Consequently, it has been the subject of more oversight than any other industry.

The financial services industry is particularly susceptible to the Y2K problem. The industry uses computers to calculate interest and mortgage payments, process stock trades and access account information. Without reliable systems, interest could be miscalculated, stock trades could vanish, and customers could have difficulty accessing their account balances or using their credit or debit cards. Such problems, even if only temporary, could create the type of uncertainty and chaos that has been responsible for major economic downturns in the past. Therefore, it is important not only to assure that the computer systems in this industry are remediated and tested, but that financial services organizations avoid consumer panic by communicating effectively with customers and business partners.

As a result of early attention to the problem and significant regulatory and Congressional oversight, the financial services sector ranks ahead of virtually all other industries in its remediation and testing efforts.

Even in this sector, however, much additional work will be required, particularly in the areas of contingency planning, and international operations and information exchange.

Major Initiatives

Regulatory Survey

In February and again in April 1997, both Senators Bennett and D'Amato cosigned letters to each of the six federal financial institution regulatory agencies asking that they provide information about the Y2K readiness of their own computer systems as well as those in the industry sectors under their supervision. The responses raised serious questions about Year 2000 readiness in the financial services sector and the Chairman decided to use the hearing process to investigate further.

Hearings

July 10, 1997: Hearing on Financial Services and the Year 2000 Problem

In the first hearing, the Subcommittee solicited testimony from a variety of individuals experienced in working with the Y2K issue. The issues raised in this first hearing would reemerge consistently throughout the following hearings.

Highlights

- Large banks started their Y2K preparations well in advance of other industry sectors. However, interdependency, industry consolidation, external vendor reliance and a greater proportion of mission-critical systems makes the financial services industry particularly susceptible to Y2K problems.

- The panel endorsed direct and immediate federal and regulatory action. The Bank Administration Institute was given as an example of how industry groups could positively support the Y2K effort. As one panelist stated, the Year 2000 has the potential of falling prey to the tragedy of the commons—it is everyone's problem, therefore few are willing to take responsibility for it.

- Businesses have a special responsibility to inform the public of their Y2K preparedness. Loss of faith by consumers in either the soundness of their investments or their financial service providers could throw the economy into turmoil even without major Y2K disruptions.

- The "silver bullet" that defeats the Y2K problem is not technology, but solid project management. This includes engaging in triage to identify mission-critical systems and contingency planning, especially in smaller institutions or those bodies that have yet to initiate Y2K remediation. Time for a complete Y2K fix is rapidly diminishing.

> *A consumer loss of faith in either the soundness of their investments or their financial service providers could throw the economy into turmoil even without major Y2K disruptions.*

Although the hearing on U.S. Financial Institutions and Federal Regulatory Agencies Management of the Year 2000 Computer Problem had already been scheduled for July 30, the July 10 hearing affirmed the Subcommittee's conclusion that regulators would play a critical role in Y2K preparedness.

July 30, 1997: Hearing on U.S. Financial Institutions, and Federal Regulatory Agencies Management of the Year 2000 Computer Problem

As a result of the letters sent by Senators D'Amato and Bennett in February and April of 1997, the heads of the six financial institution regulatory agencies were prepared to address the concerns of the Subcommittee. While the Office of Thrift Supervision (OTS) claimed it could trace Y2K concerns back to thrift examinations in 1994 and the Governors of the Federal Reserve Board (FRB) pointed to the consolidation of the FRB mainframe 5 years ago as the beginning of the FRB's Y2K awareness, most agencies started to actively engage the Y2K issue in June 1996 in response to a Federal Financial Institutions Examination Council statement. This statement "strongly encouraged depository institutions to complete an inventory of core computer functions and to set priorities for compliance changes, keeping in mind that testing should be underway for mission-critical systems by December 31, 1998." Almost a year later, in May 1997, FFIEC issued a second statement which provided some guidance for banks and examiners on Y2K project management. Another, more detailed guidance statement was issued in December 1997.

> *The "silver bullet" that defeats the Y2K problem is not technology, but solid project management.*

Highlights

- While examination information is confidential by law, the Subcommittee asked the regulators to consider ways in which they could disclose Y2K preparedness levels to the public. As a whole, the regulators' opinion fell to the side of maintaining the status quo. Defining Y2K as a safety and soundness issue, regulators argued that the examination results should remain confidential in accordance with current law. Financial institutions that fail to comply with Year 2000 regulatory guidelines will be subject to formal enforcement actions which, in contrast to examination reports, the regulators are required to publish by law. The Committee warned that information held by regulators, and not appropriately distributed to the public promptly, would increase the likelihood of panic.

> *Information not appropriately distributed to the public in a timely manner will increase the likelihood of panic.*

- The securities industry also defended its current disclosure laws, while suggesting that individual consumers and investors would most influence disclosure. Arthur Levitt, Jr. of the Securities and Exchange Commission (SEC) claimed that current laws in place were "sufficient at this time to cover reporting obligations concerning any material impact of the Year 2000 on operations or costs." Moreover, "market forces are such that there is no regulatory action that would be as severe as the reaction of the marketplace."
- Senators Bennett and Dodd presented the idea of "safe harbor" legislation that would encourage institutions to focus on fixing the Y2K problem by offering some protection from Y2K liability for companies that demonstrate Y2K due diligence. The panel was reluctant to comment on an unwritten bill, but generally indicated that self-interest should be sufficient encouragement to address Y2K problems.

While commending the agencies' excellent Y2K efforts, the senators requested regular progress reports, especially to address certain weaknesses identified in the hearing. Two such areas were the underpreparedness of small institutions and international institutions. Senator Dodd also took the occasion to disagree with the SEC's view on disclosure, stating, "by the time the market reacts . . . we may have a problem on our hands."

October 22, 1997: Hearing on the Year 2000 Liability and Disclosure

Continuing the debate on liability and disclosure that started in the previous hearing, the October 22 hearing sought the perspective of a different set of witnesses: two lawyers intimately involved in Y2K, the president of Information Technology Association of America whose constituents may have significant Y2K liability exposure, and a professional investment analyst. The Chairman considered the need to protect companies from excessive Y2K-related litigation, balanced with a concern that public companies did not adequately disclose their Y2K efforts. The Director of the Division of Corporate Finance for the SEC was asked to respond to this last criticism, especially in light of Senate Bill 1518, which would require specific Y2K disclosure for public companies.

Highlights

- Corporations could face liability risks from a range of sources at an aggregate cost of $1 trillion. The degree to which protection from litigation may be needed or warranted is unclear. Suggestions included prohibiting punitive damage awards in Y2K-related cases amending the Copyright Act to allow businesses to adapt software without acquiring licenses, and adapting a safe harbor law which would provide some liability protection upon the businesses' good faith pursuit and implementation of a Year 2000 remediation plan.

- It was reported that institutions are severely constrained from sharing Y2K-related information and possible solutions due to liability concerns. "They [businesses] are very concerned about leaving a smoking gun in the file where they may be seen as instructing another party as to what it takes to interface with their systems and, falling short, they may have missed something." (President of LaBoeuf Computing Technologies, Inc.)

- Banks and insurance agencies can pressure businesses to address Y2K issues by factoring Y2K preparedness into applications for credit or insurance coverage. Banks have started to consider Y2K risk in credit applications, but have not yet discovered a solution for Y2K exposure in their loan portfolios. Due to a soft market, Property and Casualty insurers have been much slower to factor Y2K into insurance coverage. However, reinsurers are excluding Year 2000 liability in their reinsurance treaties.

- The SEC reiterated its position that current guidelines are sufficient to compel Y2K disclosure, while acknowledging the need for further awareness. According to the SEC representative, "[t]here appears to be a problem in the sense that we aren't getting as many disclosures as we would expect . . . there is a concern that companies may not understand that this is another issue that's impacted by the federal securities laws."

The Chairman finished the hearing by informing the Subcommittee of the results of a GAO report assessing the National Credit Union Association (NCUA). The report, requested just after the previous hearing, indicated that the NCUA was not as far along in its assessment of Year 2000 compliance as the Office of Management and Budget and GAO guidelines recommended. He encouraged the NCUA to accelerate its Y2K activities, and warned the other regulatory agencies that GAO would visit them soon.

November 4, 1997: Hearing on Mandating Year 2000 Disclosure by Publicly Traded Companies
The fourth hearing of the Subcommittee featured the testimony of Edward Yardeni, Chief Economist at Deutsch Morgan Grenfell. The hearing was one of many steps taken to pressure public companies to provide greater Y2K disclosure. Yardeni, who gave an estimated 40% chance of a worldwide recession in 2000 lasting at least 12 months, felt very strongly that a new, comprehensive disclosure law was necessary. In his testimony he stated, "The current disclosure system simply will not provide policymakers with the information they need as soon as possible to anticipate and to prepare for plausible worst-case scenarios."

February 10, 1998: Hearing on FDIC's Year 2000 Preparedness
The fifth hearing of the Subcommittee provided a public forum for examining the results of GAO's assessment of the Federal Deposit Insurance Corporation's Y2K efforts. While the report noted that the FDIC had made significant strides in its Year 2000 project, it still lagged behind OMB and GAO guidelines. The FDIC acknowledged its shortcomings and provided the Subcommittee with details regarding its ongoing and future Y2K efforts. The Subcommittee discussed the idea of a "drop dead" (i.e., shutdown) date for noncompliant institutions and the need to provide customers with meaningful disclosure on their banks' Y2K readiness.

February 17, 1998: Field Hearing Implications of the Year 2000 Computer Problem
Senator Dodd chaired the sixth hearing in Hartford, Connecticut, to illustrate the breadth and pervasiveness of the Y2K problem. Seven witnesses described their Y2K programs and the implications for their customers in a variety of areas, including banking, insurance, medical facilities and airway transportation. Participants reaffirmed the interdependent nature of busi-

ness and encouraged consumers to ask their product and service providers about their Y2K efforts.

March 18, 1998: Hearing on Office of Thrift Supervision Year 2000 Preparedness

The Subcommittee heard a positive report from GAO on OTS's Y2K efforts, with particular praise directed at OTS's internal systems work. The OTS was criticized for not having completed its contingency plans, and ignoring the interrelationships between its internal systems. However, the OTS had improved on NCUA's and FDIC's initial member assessments, and therefore had a better base from which to determine its regulated entities' preparedness levels. At the time, OTS estimated less than 22% of its regulated entities "needed improvement" and around 1% were "unsatisfactory" in their Y2K efforts.

> *The SEC and other expert witnesses agreed that while the quantity of disclosures improved, the quality did not.*

During the course of the hearing the Chairman asked whether the FFIEC had become a bottleneck for information. Although the OTS representative hesitated to agree, she did mention that the OTS would issue its own testing guidance in the following weeks, and contingency planning guidance toward the end of April.

June 10, 1998: Hearing on Disclosing Year 2000 Readiness

On June 10, 1998, Chairman Bennett called the SEC back to the witness table to report on the progress of its efforts to improve Y2K disclosure among publicly traded corporations. After the introduction of Senate Bill 1518, the Computer Remediation and Shareholder (CRASH) Protection Act, the SEC requested the opportunity to address the problem of disclosure on its own, without additional legislation. In the months that followed, the SEC attempted to improve the quality of disclosure by educating publicly traded companies about their obligations under existing law. Unfortunately, the SEC's efforts were only moderately successful. The SEC and other expert witnesses agreed that while the quantity of disclosure improved, the quality did not.

Highlights

- The SEC reiterated its commitment to improving Year 2000 disclosure. It promised to heighten its efforts by releasing specific guidance on Y2K disclosure. This interpretive release "may form the basis of enforcement action regarding their Year 2000 issues," and "will remedy the apparent misconception that costs relating to fixing Year 2000 problems must be disclosed only if these costs are material. It will clarify that companies must determine materiality based on the potential consequences of their failure to resolve their Year 2000 readiness."

- Supporting the need for better disclosure, Triaxsys Research provided the Subcommittee with statistics from a survey of the largest 250 publicly held companies. As of April 17, 1998, nearly half of these companies disclosed no information, or so little information that it was impossible to glean anything meaningful about their Y2K progress. Another witness observed that the Y2K disclosure of many institutions looked as if lawyers had heavily edited them. "Clearly, corporations have violated the SEC guideline requiring specifics rather than boilerplates."

- The Subcommittee discussed the possibility of changing the incentive structure so that companies would be biased toward the disclosure of information. Disincentives, such as the use of disclosed information against a company in litigation, abound. Tying limits on Y2K liability and litigation to disclosure of information and efforts to fix a company's problem may be one way to neutralize the disincentives to disclose.

Although not directly within the scope of the Subcommittee's jurisdiction, the hearing finished with a debate on the pros and cons of providing liability protection to corporate boards and senior management. The Chairman requested that the participating legal experts avail themselves to Senator Kyl, who is the Chairman of the Judiciary Subcommittee on Technology, Terrorism, and Government Information for further discussion.

> *Clearly, corporations have violated the SEC guidelines requiring specifics rather than boilerplates.*

July 6, 1998: Field Hearing in Assessing the Year 2000 Preparedness of Foreign Countries and Determining Just Where and How the United States May Be Vulnerable

In this hearing, representatives from the U.S. financial services arena confirmed that international preparedness poses a real, but unquantified, risk to U.S. companies. Witnesses could point to such international efforts as the Joint Year 2000 Council (sponsored jointly through the Basle Committee, the G-10 Central Bank Governors' Committee on Payment and Settlement Systems, the International Association of Insurance Supervisors, and the International Organization of Securities Commissions), but little tangible information was available. The few pieces that were available were disheartening. Quoting a Moody's investment report, one witness noted that 49 Japanese banks planned to spend $249 million as a group on Y2K compliance. This amount is only a fraction of Citicorp's planned $600 million program.

September 17, 1998: Hearing on Y2K and Pensions and Mutual Funds
Since pension and mutual funds are the primary vehicle through which Americans invest in the stock market, the Committee held a hearing on fund managers' efforts to address the Year 2000 problem. The attending pension and mutual fund company representatives reported that their internal systems were well on their way to compliance. They also indicated that they were not impressed with disclosure efforts made by public companies. However, several witnesses conceded that many analysts as well as fund managers had just started to include Y2K risk in their evaluation of stocks. Additionally, they emphasized that their position required an equal evaluation of all risk. Chairman Bennett countered that the Committee had no intention of asking analysts to change their evaluation of other risks. Instead, the Chairman warned that the failure to inform stockholders of Y2K risks would result in significant long-term risks. The Committee wanted to preserve confidence in the market by ensuring that analysts recognized Y2K as an important risk.

Legislation
In the 105th Congress, Chairman Bennett introduced the following three pieces of legislation to further the goals of Year 2000 readiness in the financial services industry. Detailed summaries of the bills are found in the Legislation section of this report.

S. *1518*, the Year 2000 Computer Remediation and Shareholder (CRASH) Protection Act of 1997, was introduced on November 10, 1997.

S. *1671*, the Examination Parity and Year 2000 Readiness for Financial Institutions Act, was introduced on February 24, 1998.

S. *2000*, was introduced on April 29, 1998.

Regulatory Briefings

At the second Subcommittee hearing on July 30, 1997, Chairman Bennett asked the six federal financial institution regulatory agencies to report back to the Subcommittee on a regular basis on the progress of Year 2000 remediation in their own operations and in the industry sectors they supervise. Since that time, the Subcommittee has worked with the House Banking Committee to establish a regular schedule of quarterly briefings. Each quarter, the regulatory agencies file written reports with the Subcommittee on their progress and meet with Congressional staff to respond to questions raised by the reports.

General Accounting Office Studies

In August 1997, Chairman Bennett asked GAO to conduct an independent review of the Year 2000 remediation efforts at each of the six financial institution regulatory agencies. GAO has concluded several of those reviews and has reported back to the Chairman. The results of those reviews are incorporated, as appropriate, in the "Assessment" section of this report, as well as in the hearings where the GAO reported its findings.

Correspondence and Industry Outreach

Chairman Bennett maintains regular contact with government officials and industry representatives involved in the Year 2000 remediation and risk management processes. These contacts include both formal speeches and informal meetings. He has written op-ed pieces for the *New York Times,* involved himself heavily in the Annual Conference on Financial Services and Technology in Utah, spoken with CEOs of top technology firms at the Comdex convention, and addressed the National Press Club, among other activities. Subcommittee and Special Committee staffs meet regularly with industry representatives to continually assess progress in the sector.

Assessments

Financial Institutions and Their Regulatory Agencies

Based on GAO reports and constant contact with industry representatives, the Committee feels comfortable with progress that regulators have made in remediating and testing their internal systems. However, regulators must continue to push themselves to meet the OMB's March 1999 implementation date for their mission-critical systems.

Of the institutions evaluated under that system, approximately 95% received satisfactory ratings. Fewer than 1% of institutions received an unsatisfactory rating.

Very few institutions should fail due to lack of Y2K planning. On-site examinations performed by four of the regulators (FRB, FDIC, Office of the Comptroller of the Currency and OTS) resulted in approximately 95% of institutions surveyed receiving satisfactory ratings. Less than 1% of institutions surveyed received an unsatisfactory rating.

Smaller institutions are more likely to lag in their preparations. NCUA, which regulates a disproportionate amount of smaller institutions, reports a slightly larger percentage of unsatisfactory institutions.

The Committee is pleased that the regulators are considering the needs of consumers in their Y2K preparations. Besides an FFIEC release on Year 2000 customer awareness programs, the FRB has planned to increase the amount of currency either in circulation or in Federal Reserve vaults by approximately 14% over current levels by the end of 1999. This inflow of currency will permit financial institutions to provide the extra cash customers may demand during the century rollover.

Financial institutions have started to evaluate the Year 2000 preparedness of their material customers and include Year 2000 preparedness in their underwriting and loan review standards. This process is just beginning, however, and there are no reports of customers being rejected for loans or of loans being downgraded as a result of Year 2000 questions. The Committee will encourage the industry to pursue this analysis in the coming year.

The regulators need to develop plans for when and how they will deal with those institutions likely to experience significant failures after the millennium date change. On encouragement from the Chairman, formal enforcement actions have been taken where appropriate. In the case of the Putnam-Greene Financial Corporation, the FDIC and FRB issued coordinated cease-and-desist orders citing inadequate Y2K preparations. Continued monitoring is imperative.

The Securities Industry

The securities industry has led the financial services sector in its Year 2000 remediation efforts.

The securities industry scheduled industry-wide testing in 1999, but in July 1998, the Securities Industry Association (SIA) conducted a rehearsal or so-called "beta test." In testimony before the Special Committee on September 17, 1998, Don Kittell of the SIA reported that 28 securities firms participated in the test, along with 13 exchanges and selected utilities. The results of the testing were generally positive and the firms were able to process a complete cycle of trades over a simulated millennium date change. The Committee remains positive about these tests, although expanded testing is necessary to ensure that more firms are Y2K ready.

The SEC has made a commendable effort to promote Year 2000 preparedness within the securities industry and keep investors informed. SEC initiatives include:

- A frequently asked question sheet on the SEC's web site containing a list of frequently asked Y2K questions for investors.

- Numerous statements to publicly traded companies, broker-dealers, and investment advisers to promote disclosure of Year 2000 information. (Available at www.sec.gov.) As a result of an early and vigorous start, the securities industry is well positioned for the Year 2000.

Failures

The reality of information technology is that glitches can occur without user discovery until well after the fact. A case in point is the recent failure of a data collection company for the financial services industry. Portions of the firm's database were processed using the old MS-DOS operating system. This was not Y2K compliant. When January 1999 rolled around the system assumed "9" meant end of file, a common programmer protocol for older systems. Fund managers receiving this data encountered an array of N/As sprinkled throughout the data tables that list financial metrics such as cumulative return rates, 12-month yields and price-to-book ratios. In fact these were indications that January 1999 data were not included. The benchmark S&P 500 index was incorrect. Some customers were not notified about the problem until three weeks later. If financial decisions were made based on imprecise data, then potential negative consequences could have resulted. This example is an indication of the kind of problems that can befall the financial industry where seemingly trivial mistakes can have undesirable consequences.

Retirement and Mutual Funds

Retirement and mutual funds, though regulated by separate entities (the Pension and Welfare Benefits Administration [PWBA] and the SEC, respectively), face similar Y2K problems. Testimony before the Special Committee revealed that both groups have focused more on preparing their own internal systems than evaluating their external exposure.

Some pension and mutual fund plans have undertaken comprehensive Y2K-specific surveys of the companies in which they invest. However, many others have been slow to incorporate Y2K exposure into their evaluation of investments.

The Committee recognizes that regulators have not been silent on the Y2K issue for pension and mutual fund providers. Initiatives include the following:

- PWBA published a pamphlet entitled, "Fiduciary Questions and Answers about the Year 2000." (Available at 1-800-998-7542 or www.dol.gov/dol/pwba.)
- The SEC has worked with the Investment Company Institute (ICI) to monitor progress. An ICI survey revealed that 80% of responding mutual fund companies expected to finish internal remediation by year end 1998.

In third quarter results tabulated by the SEC, 10% of 15,000 companies failed to disclose their year 2000 costs.

However, considerably more effort is necessary to convince investment advisers from both groups that portfolios should be examined for Y2K risk, and that Y2K risk should be disclosed to underlying investors.

An investment in a company that may not be Year 2000 compliant could be detrimental to plan participants and consequently expose the plan fiduciary to liability. Therefore, the Special Committee has urged all pension plans to evaluate their investments.

Publicly Traded Corporations

The Committee is disappointed to report that despite substantial improvement in the number of public companies now mentioning Y2K in their SEC disclosures, very few companies have provided the type of meaningful disclosure necessary to assess the potential impact of Y2K on their business.

Having studied the problem, the Committee agrees with economist Edward Yardeni, who testified that the Year 2000 problem would have a material impact on companies that do not make adequate Y2K preparations.

While data suggests that many U.S. companies, especially large corporations, are working diligently to address their Y2K issues, companies appear to be avoiding Y2K disclosure by taking the position that either 1) Y2K will not have a material impact on them, 2) it is too early to assess the possible impact of Y2K failures, 3) such disclosure would reveal proprietary information and/or place them at a disadvantage against competitors, or 4) their counsel had advised them to share as little information as possible while still complying with the letter of the law.

Whether the situation will improve in the remaining reporting periods remains unclear. Failing to address Y2K exposure could have a disastrous effect on a company, and further pressure may be needed to ensure that public companies disclose that risk to investors.

Concerns

International

Financial services firms in the United States are linked closely to their counterparts in other parts of the world through electronic transactions. U.S. firms operating around the world also must rely on telecommunications and power services in foreign countries in order to transact business. As a result, even if U.S. financial services firms have converted their own systems successfully, they still face enormous international risk. Experts testifying before the Subcommittee and Special Committee consistently have stressed that while there is much uncertainty

about Year 2000 readiness around the world, one fact is clear—
most foreign countries lag behind the U.S. in their conversion
activities.

Senator Bennett has urged financial services firms and their
regulators to assess the Year 2000 situation of the countries in
which they operate and to develop contingency plans to mitigate the effects of failure in those jurisdictions. The Special
Committee also has asked the GAO to assess the Year 2000 situation abroad. That study is ongoing at this time.

Contingency Planning

With their remediation efforts on track, financial services companies must now address the more complex issue of contingency planning. Firms have been slow to address this issue as a
result of competing priorities and the lack of meaningful information about the Year 2000 readiness of outside companies and
other sectors. Nevertheless, financial services firms and their
regulators must plan for how they will maintain their operations if unexpected failures occur. Financial services firms are
particularly vulnerable to power or telecommunications failures as well as to the risk that a material customer or business
partner will fail, as a result of the computer problems, to meet
its obligations. The Special Committee plans to question financial services firms about their contingency planning efforts in
1999.

Disclosure

Promoting meaningful disclosure of companies' Year 2000
readiness has been the cornerstone of Senator Bennett's efforts.
Without meaningful disclosure, it is impossible for firms to
properly assess their own risks and develop necessary contingency plans. Disclosure is also important in the context of congressional oversight. The Special Committee will continue to
promote this important goal in 1999.

Cost

According to disclosure reports filed by financial services firms in recent months, the costs of Year 2000 compliance are rising. Most companies have found that while the cost of remediation has flattened out, the costs of contingency planning exceed their estimates. Based on these results, it is possible that the cost of remediation could have a negative impact on earnings in the financial services sector. Depressed earnings in the financial services sector could adversely impact the U.S. economy.

Third Party Relationships

While financial services companies lead many other industries in the conversion and testing of their own systems, they are just beginning to assess and manage the risks attributable to third party relationships. Financial institutions must assess the Year 2000 readiness of their material customers in order to avoid suffering major loan losses. Mutual funds and pension funds must consider the readiness of their portfolio companies in order to guard against unnecessary and foreseeable losses and shield themselves from the liability associated with those losses. The process of examining the Year 2000 preparedness of third parties has been hindered somewhat by the lack of substantive disclosure. The SEC's Interpretive Ruling and the passage of the Information Readiness and Disclosure Act should make the information necessary for such an analysis more available.

Security

Financial service providers have shipped massive quantities of code to overseas correcting facilities. In the process, core legacy systems have been mapped and documented. This brings some real benefit to institutions that may have otherwise been ignorant of the inner workings of their own systems. Unfortunately, it also provides the opportunity for unscrupulous individuals to learn about the inner workings of corporations' security systems.

Additionally, the Committee is concerned about the potential for code tampering during the remediation process. A British computer society claims that some code returned from overseas processing already has been found to contain "trap doors," or secret electronic entry points into a computer system. Trap doors could be implanted by programmers during Y2K remediation and then accessed at a later date, once the unsuspecting company is running on its new, "cleaned" data.

General Government

Emergency Preparedness

Overview

When an individual is confronted by a personal emergency in the United States, he or she can be confident that any 911 call for assistance will be answered promptly, and that a competent authority will respond rapidly. Y2K presents two essential threats to our emergency service and disaster preparedness agencies. First, it threatens to interrupt the ability to properly process and respond to calls for assistance. This threat is present at all levels, from the potential interruption to a citizen's call for fire or police assistance to delays in a state's ability to request emergency or disaster assistance from the federal government. Second, due to lack of experience with anything like the possible affects of the disruptions we may face, it presents a novel challenge to those who must devise Y2K emergency response strategies unlike those they have formulated in the past.

Most 911 emergency dispatch centers, known as Public Safety Answering Points (PSAP), are highly automated, particularly in the case of enhanced 911 systems. Enhanced 911 systems are those which automatically provide the caller's location and phone number to the 911 operator. According to the FCC, the Association of Public Safety Communications Officials (APCO) has identified 50 pieces of equipment within a PSAP that have Y2K vulnerabilities. There are approximately 4,500 PSAPs located throughout the United States.

Modern emergency dispatch facilities often incorporate sophisticated Computer-Aided Dispatch (CAD) systems into their operations. CAD systems provide important benefits to public safety communication systems, including:

> *"There are certain things that can spawn panic, and panic doesn't help preparation. We need to prepare, not panic."*
>
> Senator Gordon Smith

- improved call-taking service to the public,
- provision of greater accuracy, efficiency, and speed in responding to calls for service,
- enhanced officer safety by providing detailed information on call locations, and
- increased officer productivity and resource management and provision of additional system capacity due to growth or crisis.

CAD systems are especially vulnerable to Year 2000 problems due to the fact that they perform time and date calculations on the time an initial call for assistance was received, when a unit was dispatched, the time that it arrived and how long it took to resolve the emergency. These systems are in widespread use in all areas of local emergency service, including police, fire and emergency medical services (EMS).

Sophisticated information technology systems serve as important tools for emergency service agencies today, particularly for law enforcement. Systems such as the National Crime

Information Center (NCIC), the National Law Enforcement Telecommunications System (NLETS), Automated Fingerprint Identification Systems (AFIS) and individual criminal information data systems operated individually by all 50 states enable officers to obtain the most up-to-date information on wanted persons, stolen vehicles, criminal histories, and department of motor vehicle records. The ability to access this information dependably and quickly is essential both to officer safety and to the speedy and effective administration of justice at all levels. A recent survey conducted on the effectiveness of NCIC indicates that during a one year period, 81,750 wanted persons were found, 113,293 individuals were arrested, 39,268 missing juveniles and 8,549 missing adults were located and 110,681 stolen cars valued at over $570 million were recovered as a result of NCIC's use.

The Federal Bureau of Investigation (FBI) is responsible for the administration of NCIC and has assured the Committee staff that this system will fully meet its Year 2000 challenge, successfully maintaining its links to the systems of all 50 states. The challenge for local law enforcement agencies is to be sure that their own links to NCIC and NLETS via state maintained connections and any other similar systems operated on a regional or agency-wide level are compliant and compatible with the larger systems. Also, at the local agency level, there often is a great deal of "interconnectivity" between the emergency service department's systems and those of other city agencies, such as the court system, the corrections department, and even local utility companies, thereby increasing the potential for Y2K-related problems in this area.

As is true in other areas, Y2K's presence is insidious in the area of emergency services. One major police department related to the Committee staff that its city's government was required to remediate its gasoline pumps in order to ensure that gasoline would continue to flow to its patrol cars on January 1, 2000. This problem had the potential to affect the entire fleet of city government-owned vehicles. In this particular case, the computerized gasoline pumps perform a time and date calculation based upon the last time a particular gas credit card was used to fuel a vehicle and therefore the pumps were Y2K vulnerable.

In another case, the sheriff of a large western county related that his department was currently examining its computerized detention files which track in and out time of inmates at the county jail facility and hearing date information for inmates. Additionally, a consultant specializing in Y2K public safety problems provided the Committee staff with a list of over 35 items of technical equipment commonly used in law enforcement that could potentially be vulnerable to embedded chip problems. These items included patrol car mounted video equipment, mobile data systems and electronic prisoner monitoring devices used in home detention and probation.

In addition to the technical aspect of Y2K vulnerabilities, emergency service departments must also consider the possibility that January 1, 2000, may bring with it an enormous increase in the demand for their services, depending on the degree of disruption experienced. This must be considered as part of Year 2000 emergency planning at the state, county, and local levels of government.

U.S. Emergency Services Structure

The U.S. emergency service and disaster response sector is a multilayered safety net consisting of local, county, and state police departments, local and county fire departments, emergency medical service agencies, local, county, and state emergency management organizations, volunteer organizations and a coordinated network of federal resources available when state and local resources are exhausted or overrun. The Y2K problem bears the potential to affect all layers and sections of this safety net. In the event of serious Y2K-related disruptions, many of the organizations that comprise the safety net will be called upon to respond.

According to the Bureau of Justice Statistics, there are over 17,000 police and sheriffs departments in the U.S. The International Association of Fire Chiefs estimates that there are 32,000 fire departments in this country. Additionally, approximately 65% of our country's EMS agencies reside within the organizational structure of our nation's fire departments.

Statistics provided by the National Emergency Number Association indicate that over 300,000 911 emergency calls are placed in this country daily. (Approximately 110 million calls for emergency assistance per year.) An additional 83,000 calls for emergency assistance are placed via cellular phones. Ninety percent of the U.S. population is covered by 911 service.

Each of the 50 states and U.S. territories encompass an emergency management department headed by a state emergency manager. The governors in each respective state appoint many of these managers. The emergency manager serves as the chief disaster preparedness and response coordinator in the state. Twenty-four states and one U.S. territory are currently signatories to the Emergency Management Assistance Compact. The Compact provides for mutual assistance between the states in managing any disaster or emergency that is duly declared by the governor of the affected state, whether arising from natural disaster, technological hazard, man-made disaster, resource shortages, community disorders, insurgency or enemy attack. This compact also provides for mutual cooperation in emergency-related exercises, testing, or other training activities. While on its face it would appear that this compact would hold the promise of being well-suited to address the many problems that may arise from the Year 2000 problem, discussions with a number of emergency managers reveals otherwise. During her testimony before the Committee on October 2, 1998, Ms. Ellen Gordon, President of the National Emergency Managers Association (NEMA), explained that mutual aid between the states might not be possible in the event that all states are affected in a significant manner.

Individual states might not be able to spare limited resources or be in a position to lend other mutual aid. One state emergency manager told Committee staff that he would be hesitant to release any of his own resources to another state because of the degree of uncertainty about potential Y2K disruptions.

The Federal Emergency Management Agency (FEMA) was established in June 1979 by President Carter to improve the responsiveness of the federal government to catastrophes in the United States. FEMA provides financial and technical assistance to states and localities overwhelmed by disasters. FEMA administers policies related to emergency management and planning, evacuation, and matters associated with civil defense, disaster relief, fire prevention, earthquake hazard reduction, emergency broadcasting services, flood insurance, mitigation programs and dam safety. The principal federal authority for the provision of disaster relief is the Robert T. Stafford Disaster Relief and Emergency Assistance Act (the Stafford Act). The act authorizes the President to issue major disaster or emergency declarations, sets out eligibility criteria and specifies the types of assistance the President may authorize. Aid is provided to meet urgent housing needs, purchase necessary personal items and obtain legal services needed as a result of disasters. Aid is provided to state and local governments and non-profit organizations to repair or reconstruct damaged or destroyed infrastructure, remove debris and to construct protective measures. In addition to the assistance provided by the Stafford Act, federal disaster assistance is also provided by other federal agencies (see description of the Federal Plan).

The Federal Response Plan [1]

The Federal Response Plan (the Stafford Act) established the authority for the federal government to respond to disasters and emergencies in order to provide assistance to save lives and protect public health, safety, and property. It is applicable to natural disasters such as earthquakes, hurricanes, typhoons, tornadoes and volcanic eruptions; technological emergencies involving radiological or hazardous material releases; and other incidents requiring federal assistance.

The Plan establishes the architecture for a systematic, coordinated and effective federal response to disasters or other emergencies. It concentrates the provision of federal assistance a state is most likely to need under 12 Emergency Support Functions (ESF). Each ESF is headed by a primary agency, which has been selected based on its authorities, resources, and capabilities. The 12 ESFs are the primary mechanism through which federal response assistance is provided to the affected state.

Emergency Support Functions

ESF #1—*Transportation:* U.S. Department of Transportation

ESF #2—*Communication:* U.S. National Communications System

ESF #3—*Public Works and Engineering:* U.S. Department of Defense

ESF #4—*Firefighting:* U.S. Department of Agriculture

ESF #5—*Information and Planning:* FEMA

ESF #6—*Mass Care:* American Red Cross

ESF #7—*Resource Support:* General Services Administration

ESF #8—*Health and Medical Services:* U.S. Department of Health Human Services

ESF #9—*Urban Search and Rescue:* U.S. Department of Defense

ESF #10—*Hazardous Materials:* Environmental Protection Agency

ESF #11—*Food:* U.S. Department of Agriculture

ESF #12—*Energy:* U.S. Department of Energy

The Plan describes federal actions to be taken in providing immediate response assistance to one or more affected states.[2] Response assistance includes those actions and activities which support state and local government efforts to save lives, protect public health and safety, and protect property. In some instances, a disaster or emergency may result in a situation that affects the national security of the United States. In those instances, other national security authorities and procedures could be used.

Each state has general responsibility for law enforcement, using local and state resources, including the National Guard. In some cases, a state government may experience a law enforcement emergency (including one in connection with a disaster or emergency) in which it is unable to adequately respond. For example, it may be an uncommon situation that requires law enforcement assistance, one that is or threatens to become of serious or epidemic (large-scale) proportions, and one in which state and local resources are inadequate to protect lives and property of citizens or to enforce the criminal law. In the event such a law enforcement emergency exists throughout a state or part of a state (on behalf of itself or a local unit of government), the governor may, in accordance with the Federal Response Plan, request emergency federal law enforcement assistance from the U.S. Attorney General. If the request is approved, federal law enforcement assistance may be provided to include equipment, training, intelligence or personnel.

Our national security is dependent upon our ability to assure continuity of government, at every level, in any national security emergency situation that might confront the nation. Executive Order 12656, the Assignment of Emergency Preparedness Responsibilities, broadly outlines the role of FEMA's director and the National Security Council in response to national security emergencies. Executive Order 12656 defines a national security emergency as "any occurrence, including natural disaster, military attack, technological emergency or other emergency, that seriously degrades or seriously threatens the national security of the United States." It establishes the role of the President in national security emergency preparedness. Pursuant to the President's direction, the National Security Council is responsible for developing and administering our national security policy.

Our national security policy dictates that all national security emergency preparedness activities shall be consistent with the Constitution and laws of the United States and with preservation of the constitutional government of the United States.

Effective national security emergency preparedness planning requires identification of the functions that would have to be performed during such an emergency, development of plans for performing these functions and development of the capability to execute those plans.

Executive Order 12656 establishes that the director of FEMA shall serve as an adviser to the National Security Council on issues of national security emergency preparedness, including mobilization preparedness, civil defense, continuity of government, technological disasters, and other issues, as appropriate. It also states that the director of FEMA also shall assist in the implementation of national security emergency preparedness policy by coordinating with the other federal departments and agencies and with state and local governments, and by providing periodic reports to the National Security Council.

The public has voiced its concern to the Committee regarding the role that the federal government will play in responding to Y2K-related emergencies. Numerous misguided rumors and outright falsehoods are being circulated in some quarters on the Internet about the possibility that "martial law" will somehow be declared by the federal government in response to Y2K emergencies. These rumors and falsehoods will serve only to incite unwarranted public panic and to needlessly heighten public fear and misunderstanding about the Y2K problem. Such irresponsible and reckless speculation has no basis in fact, and it disregards the long history of our nation's commitment to democracy and our own constitutional system of government, which is grounded in the rule of law.

As the aforementioned information illustrates, a well coordinated, preexisting network exists through which appropriate emergency or disaster assistance may be rendered from the federal government down through the states and local governments when the states request such assistance. Such assistance is rendered within the context of existing legal authority, and in accordance with preexisting structures as previously described. The Committee strongly believes the emergency and disaster response structures as described within this report to be the appropriate mechanism through which any necessary federal response to Y2K-related disruptions would be provided.

Major Initiatives

On October 2, 1998, the Committee held a hearing to assess the Year 2000 readiness of government at the federal, state, and local level to continue to provide without interruption vital emergency services, such as police, fire and emergency medical services. The Committee also inquired into the ability of emergency response personnel to respond to potential Year 2000-related disruptions, such as interruptions or anomalies in the utility, communications and transportation sectors.

The hearing examined the role of FEMA in coordinating the execution of the Federal Response Plan, and the role the Plan could play in mounting a federal response to potential Y2K-related interruptions. Also, it explored the extent to which FEMA has considered potential Year 2000 disruptions as events that might require a coordinated federal response.

The hearing examined the state of FEMA's readiness to carry out its mandate under the Stafford Act in light of the Year 2000 problem and focused on FEMA's outreach to the state emergency preparedness agencies and non-governmental organizations that help respond to disasters.

Lacy Suiter, Executive Associate Director of FEMA's Response and Recovery Directorate, provided testimony about the state of FEMA's internal Y2K preparedness, its outreach to state and local emergency management and emergency services agencies, and FEMA's plans to coordinate the federal response to Y2K-induced emergencies.

FEMA's other Y2K initiatives, as described both in Mr. Suiter's written statement and testimony before this Committee are summarized as follows:

- FEMA is working with other agencies in the emergency services sector to develop an outreach plan that will include meetings on Y2K convened by federal agencies, outside meetings that federal officials will attend to increase Y2K awareness, and other communications on Y2K such as letters, public notices, web site information, and brochures. FEMA plans to post this information on its web page.

- The United States Fire Administration, which reports to FEMA, has initiated a multi-phased plan to raise awareness and assess readiness on the Y2K technology problem. The Fire Administration staff issued a suggested article for the fire and emergency services publications on Y2K preparedness, and FEMA has developed a list of frequently asked questions about Y2K in a Y2K brochure. FEMA has distributed the brochure to participants in the National Fire Academy, major fire service organizations, and state fire marshals. FEMA is in the process of conducting a direct mailing of the brochure to approximately 32,000 individual fire departments nationwide. FEMA has also distributed materials to associations of fire and emergency service equipment manufacturers and distributors requesting information on actions their members are taking to ensure that their products are Y2K compliant.

- FEMA is pursuing outreach activities with state and local governments through the National Emergency Management Association (NEMA) and the International Association of Emergency Managers (IAEM). The focus has been to heighten awareness of state and local government about the seriousness of the problem and to provide Y2K emergency preparedness guidance and information.

- NEMA has identified Y2K as a priority area and has initiated a Y2K dialogue with its members. NEMA has assigned its Preparedness, Training, and Exercises Committee to review and coordinate efforts with FEMA. FEMA is working in partnership with NEMA, IAEM and other organizations to develop preparedness guidance for the entire emergency preparedness community.
- FEMA's regional directors have been asked to contact the state emergency management directors in their region to reinforce the importance of preparedness and compliance at the state level, to emphasize the necessity of state outreach to local governments, and to help identify areas where additional assistance is needed.
- FEMA's Emergency Management Institute has incorporated a "Y2K Show-of-Hands Survey" to gauge the level of Y2K awareness of its participants.
- In November 1998, FEMA's associate director for preparedness, training, and exercises addressed the IAEM 46th Annual Conference in Norfolk, Virginia, to urge local emergency managers to participate in Y2K preparedness activities.
- FEMA is in the process of planning a series of regional "table-top" exercises to ascertain the needs of the states resulting from a Y2K-related emergency.
- FEMA will coordinate a nationwide "table top" exercise some time in the spring of 1999 to conduct an operational simulation of its response to a Y2K emergency.
- FEMA is hosting monthly meetings with primary Federal Response Plan agencies to monitor progress on the Y2K compliance status of the 12 emergency support functions.

- FEMA is developing a "Y2K Supplement" to the Federal
  Response Plan based on input from the Federal Response
  Plan agencies and their regional counterparts. Assessments from the emergency services sector and the President's Council on Y2K conversion will influence the
  composition of the supplement. FEMA plans to publish
  the supplement by July 1, 1999. The supplement will
  include a basic plan and annexes for each of the emergency support functions.

Beginning in July 1998, the Committee staff began discussions
with FEMA to determine what authority the federal government
would have to act in case of serious Y2K disruptions, and how
FEMA specifically plans to respond in the event that such disruptions do occur. In his testimony, Mr. Suiter emphasized that
FEMA programs represent a "bottoms up" approach in which
federal response comes "by invitation only," upon a specific
request from the governor of an individual state, in response to
specific and identifiable emergencies and disasters. This
response is requested by and coordinated through the governor,
and never independently by the federal government. This fact is
in stark contrast to some of the reckless assertions appearing on
the Internet, claiming that Y2K events would serve as an
"excuse" for a massive marshaling of federal forces or the sus-
pension of civil legal authority to deal with possible disruptions.

Sufficient legal authority currently exists under the Stafford
Act to allow federal resources to be utilized in response to a
Y2K-related disruption if, upon application from a state's governor, an "emergency declaration" is made by the President of
the United States. While FEMA has no authority to respond to
the causes of Y2K disruptions or to provide technical assistance
for "Y2K fixes," it can respond to the physical consequences of
Y2K disruptions if they constitute a threat to lives, property,
public health and safety pursuant to the President's "emergency
declaration."

Although FEMA cannot respond to requests for technology support, it could use the federal response system to provide a backup network to ensure that requests for such aid from state and local governments are channeled to the appropriate public/private coordination entities established by the President's Council on Y2K Conversion. FEMA currently has no plans to pre-position resources prior to January 1, 2000, but will activate the interagency Emergency Support Team at FEMA headquarters and its 10 interagency Regional Operations Centers, beginning on December 29, 1999, and continuing through January 4, 2000. FEMA will also place on alert its Emergency Response Support Detachments during that time.

Other Y2K Emergency Services Initiatives

During the summer of 1998, Federal Communications Commission Commissioner Michael Powell began playing a very active role in promoting awareness about potential Y2K-related communications problems in the public safety community. Commissioner Powell authored an article entitled "Protecting Public Safety Communications from the Year 2000 Bug," which was published in the bulletin of the Association of Public Safety Communications Officers International. In June, the FCC held a public safety roundtable which attracted many experts in the field of public safety communications. During the International Association of Chiefs of Police (IACP) Conference held in Salt Lake City October 17-22, 1998, John Clark, FCC deputy chief for public safety in the Wireless Telecommunications Bureau, addressed the major city police chiefs on Y2K issues. On November 16, 1998, the FCC sponsored a forum entitled "Year 2000: Maintaining Emergency Response Communications." The goal of the forum was to examine the implications of the Y2K problem for various segments of the emergency response communications system.

The State of Texas sponsored a 2 day national conference on

October 15 and 16, 1998, for correctional facilities, law enforcement, and emergency services on the topic of the Year 2000 and embedded systems.

In his written statement to the Committee, Sergeant John Powell, University of California Police Department, Berkeley, California, detailed several initiatives that the Association of Public Safety Communications Officials International (APCO) and the IACP are conducting on Y2K. Sergeant Powell reported that APCO and the National Institute of Justice were discussing the development of a series of short Y2K seminars targeted at public safety chief officers and upper-level management to address four key Y2K impact areas. These areas are internal systems; potential disruption of outside services such as power, 911 service, and supply chain interruptions; the additional workload that could confront agencies due to heightened fears about the problem and the advent of the actual problem itself; and the special needs of agency employees during the time of impact.

During its August 1998 conference in Albuquerque, New Mexico, APCO conducted Y2K seminars to address the broad array of issues confronting public safety agencies. The IACP Communications and Technology Committee included Y2K on its agenda at the IACP conference this year.

First Alert System

In preparing for the October 2, 1998, Hearing on General Government/Emergency Services, the Committee staff formulated the concept of a Year 2000 problem early-warning system dubbed the "Y2K First Alert." Similar to the National Weather Service's storm warning and monitoring system, the Y2K First Alert would provide American citizens with the earliest possible warning of Y2K events that may threaten public safety or national infrastructure. Senators Bennett, Dodd, and Collins jointly expressed their support for the development of this concept during the opening remarks of the October 2, 1998, hearing.

First Alert would give citizens of the eastern United States up to 17 hours advanced warning of the effects of the Year 2000. Other Americans will have proportionately more warning the farther west they live. For example, citizens in Utah will have up to 19 hours of advanced notice while citizens of Hawaii and some citizens of Alaska will have almost a full day's notice. This system would be most useful for problems that occur at or very near midnight, December 31, 1999, which could be referred to as Y2K "prompt effects." These effects could occur in embedded systems in utilities, transportation, telecommunications and other applications that had not been repaired. They could also occur in mainframe or information technology systems that serve a control or supervisory role that had not been fixed. When the century change occurs, a Y2K prompt effect may very quickly cause problems that might lead to some disruption of an important service.

The Y2K First Alert concept is feasible because of the arrangement of international time zones. A new day begins in the middle of the Pacific Ocean, 17 time zones earlier than Eastern Standard Time in the United States. If the Y2K bug is potent enough to cause immediate problems or "prompt effects" in information systems and embedded chips, the effect will not occur worldwide all at once. Rather, the problems will happen repeatedly in one time zone after another for one full day. For example, Y2K problems that occur at precisely 12:00 A.M. on January 1, 2000, in Wellington, New Zealand, are occurring while it is still only 7:00 A.M. on December 31, 1999, in the eastern United States. Systems and technology vulnerable to Y2K prompt effects in the eastern United States will not be affected for another 17 hours by the century rollover.

The Committee believes it is imperative to use this advance notice that the United States has for the good of the nation. For instance, it would be very useful to know that utility and transportation problems are likely to occur based on our Y2K First Alert system before large segments of the population are away from their homes celebrating on New Year's Eve. The Committee has called for the government to implement this concept by coordinating the resources of the Departments of State and Defense as well as other departments and federal agencies that have resources and expertise to contribute to the system.

Since the Committee issued its call on October 2, 1998, several parties have acted. FEMA has begun exploring the implementation of the concept. The telecommunications industry has begun developing a similar, private-sector concept named "Follow the Sun," and it now appears that the U.S. Air Force is pursing a related concept to meet its mission needs. Finally, the Canadian government announced in January 1999 that it plans to implement a similar concept.

Assessments

In accordance with the President's Council on the Year 2000 outreach program, the U.S. Fire Administration has been charged with monitoring the progress of the fire response agencies. Outreach to the law enforcement sector of public safety has been assigned to the Department of Justice.

While there was a high level of Y2K awareness among the limited number of representatives of individual emergency service agencies contacted by the Committee staff in preparation for the October 2, 1998, hearing, the major emergency service professional associations were just beginning to coordinate Y2K awareness programs. During her opening remarks to the International Association of Chiefs of Police Conference in Salt Lake City, Utah, in October 1998, Attorney General Janet Reno made no mention of Y2K. Some federal agencies that have regular contact with state and local criminal justice agencies were just beginning to promote awareness about the Y2K problem among the state and local agencies. The National Institute of Justice and the Bureau of Justice Assistance reported no specific or focused Y2K initiatives in progress as of the October 2, 1998, hearing. The National Institute of Justice reported that it was in the process of developing a Y2K awareness bulletin, and that it had incorporated a Y2K compliance stipulation into its grant agreements with state and local agencies.

As part of the Justice Department charged with outreach to the law enforcement community under the President's Council, both the National Institute of Justice and the Bureau of Justice Assistance could be playing a more active role in spreading Y2K awareness among state and local law enforcement and other criminal justice agencies. These agencies have a broad range of contact with criminal justice and law enforcement organizations at the state and local level of government and bear the potential to make a positive impact on the Y2K problem in the emergency service sector. As the available survey data indicates, there is a startling lack of preparedness at the state and local levels of government. All efforts to alleviate this problem should be pursued.

Almost all of the command-level emergency service personnel contacted by the Committee staff expressed serious concerns about a perceived lack of Y2K awareness on the part of emergency service agencies in general. To date, there has been no known large scale attempt to gather any meaningful survey data to measure the overall level of awareness or preparedness of this vital sector.

Concerns

While it is clear that an effective mechanism exists at the federal level to coordinate resources in the event of Y2K related emergencies or disruptions, there is still concern about the Y2K awareness and preparedness levels of emergency service providers at the county and local levels. The strong leadership role that FEMA has recently assumed in the area of Y2K emergency preparedness should have a positive impact on the state and local emergency management network and hence on the nation's overall ability to respond adequately to Y2K-related emergencies. The overall Y2K preparedness status of state and local emergency service agencies remains unknown, as does the extent to which these agencies have considered Y2K as an event for which they must creatively plan.

In his testimony before the Committee, Mr. Bob Cass, city manager of Lubbock, Texas, described the Y2K emergency simulation exercise that Lubbock had conducted just 2 days prior to the date of the Senate hearing. This exercise gained major nationwide media attention and served as an excellent example of the type of emergency planning activity that local, county and state governments should replicate. Bruce Romer, Chief Administrative Officer of Montgomery County, Maryland, also testified about Montgomery County's plans to conduct a similar exercise in December 1998. Mr. Romer has stated to the Committee staff that Montgomery County plans to activate its Emergency Operations Center prior to December 31, 1999, and said that in the event of a Y2K emergency, he "doesn't want to be looking around for people they will need." Both Lubbock, Texas, and Montgomery County, Maryland, represent model cases of effective Y2K emergency preparation.

In his written statement to the Committee, Sergeant Powell emphasized the difficulty of accommodating the additional demand for emergency services that may accompany the century date change, due in part to the possible increase in public fear toward the end of 1999. Of great concern to the Committee is the need for effective dissemination of credible information to the general public about the expected level of severity of Y2K disruptions. Governments at all levels must work constantly over the next year to obtain accurate information in order to dispel irrational and unwarranted fears about the potential impact of Y2K disruptions.

Federal Agencies

Overview

On the whole, federal agencies have been slow out of the gate in the race to cross the finish line for Y2K efforts. In this race, even though one agency or another may at times lead the pack, all agencies must cross the finish line together in a tie. As the race enters the home stretch, agencies must pick up the pace and sense of urgency. Although much progress has been made this year, the home stretch of this course is daunting.

As expected, those that started the earliest generally lead the pack. The Social Security Administration and Small Business Administration are notable agencies in front that started in the late 1980s. Considering the lead these agencies have over those that started in 1996, one can only conclude that late starters face a formidable task. The most notable agencies that have found themselves in that unenviable position include the Departments of Energy, Defense, and Health and Human Services.

All federal agencies are addressing the problem via a five-phased process: awareness, assessment, renovation, validation, and implementation. The next milestone occurs in January 1999 when agencies should complete the validation phase. The last milestone, completion of implementation, occurs in March 1999. Due to the tremendous scope and pervasiveness of potential Y2K problems, federal agencies have managed the problem through a triage process. They have identified those systems that are "mission-critical" to their ability to perform core capabilities. This triage process is deceptively complicated due to the interconnectedness of today's systems. The total effort comes down to risk management, mitigation, and avoidance.

Although agencies are focused on mission-critical systems, many other systems are too important to be completely ignored. These systems are being tracked and actively worked on at a lower priority, according to agencies' reports.

Major Initiatives

General Accounting Office

GAO has developed and published three guides that address the Y2K problem. These guides are available at www.gao.gov/Y2Kr.htm. A short description of each follows:

- The first guide, *Year 2000 Computing Crisis: An Assessment Guide,* was published in September 1997. This guide walks step-by-step through the five-phase process and provides a program assessment checklist.
- An exposure draft of the *Year 2000 Computing Crisis: A Testing Guide* was released in June 1998 and was published in November 1998. This guide provides a Y2K testing step-by-step framework. As with the conversion model described in the first guide, the test model consists of five steps: testing infrastructure, software unit testing, software integration testing, system acceptance testing and end-to-end testing.
- The final guide in the series, *Year 2000 Computing Crisis: Business Continuity and Contingency Planning,* was published in August 1998. This guide recognizes that not all systems will be fully remediated through the five-phase process before there is a Y2K impact. Additionally, as always, the unexpected and unanticipated must be planned for even when systems have completed all five phases of remediation. An excerpt from the guide notes, "Every federal agency must ensure the continuity of its core business processes by identifying, assessing, managing and mitigating its Year 2000 risks. This effort should not be limited to the risks posed by Year 2000-induced failures of internal information systems, but must include the potential Year 2000 failures of others, including business partners and infrastructure service providers." The structure described in this guide covers

four phases: initiation, business impact analysis, contingency planning and testing.

Emergency Supplemental Funding

Included in the Omnibus Consolidated and Emergency Supplemental Appropriations Act, 1999, Public Law 105-277, were provisions for $2.25 billion for non-defense agencies and activities. The Department of Defense received a separate allocation of $1.1 billion. These monies are to remain available until September 30, 2001. The purpose of these funds is to provide for expenses necessary to ensure that the information technology that is used or acquired by the federal government meets the definition of Year 2000 compliant and to meet other criteria for Year 2000 compliance as the head of each department or agency considers appropriate.

At the time this report was written, two submissions for release of emergency supplemental funds for non-defense agencies and activities had been made: November 6, 1998, and December 8, 1998. The total amount identified in these submissions is $1.23 billion, $891 million and $338 million respectively. This accounts for almost 55% of the total emergency funds available for non-defense agencies and activities. The Department of Defense has yet to submit any documentation for release of any of its $1.1 billion emergency funds for Y2K.

House Committee on Government Reform's Subcommittee on Government Management, Information, and Technology and the House Committee on Science's Subcommittee on Technology

During the 104th Congress, the House held the first hearings to review and investigate the federal government's preparedness for Y2K. Its efforts have provided critical oversight and stimulation of agency efforts. To have the broadest impact possible, both Senators Bennett and Dodd consciously narrowed our

Committee's primary focus to concentrate on the private sector and those federal agencies that provide a service to crosscutting segments of the private sector. Detailed information on Representatives Horn's and Morella's activities is found at:

- www.house.gov/reform/gmit/ and
- www.house.gov/science/Y2K.htm.

Office of Management and Budget

OMB is responsible for monitoring agency progress and efforts in addressing Y2K. Its strategy to ensure agency Y2K compliance is based on agency accountability. Progress is monitored through agency goals for compliance of mission-critical systems, progress on the status of mission-critical systems, status of mission-critical systems being repaired, and agency Y2K cost estimates. Progress reporting of federal agencies is on a quarterly and/or monthly basis depending on the tier that the agency is assigned to by OMB. The three-tier system that OMB is using consists of

Tier 1 agencies: *NOT making adequate progress,*
Tier 2 agencies: *making progress, but with concerns,* and
Tier 3 agencies: *making satisfactory progress.*

Subsequent to agency submission of quarterly status reports to OMB, OMB generates a consolidated report based on agency self-reported information. OMB's 7th Quarterly Report was issued on December 8, 1998. It is based on data as of November 15, 1998.

Efforts by OMB to provide oversight are often augmented by internal audit organizations within agencies and by GAO.

CIO Council Subcommittee on Year 2000

Among the Federal Government's Y2K initiatives, formation of the Chief Information Officers (CIO) Council Subcommittee on Year 2000, formerly the Year 2000 Interagency Committee, is the oldest. The committee was born in November 1995 when it held its first meeting. The Year 2000 Interagency Committee was an informal committee headed by Kathy Adams from the Social Security Administration. The Committee's purpose was to raise Y2K awareness, address crosscutting issues affecting many or all federal departments or agencies, seek mutual solutions where possible and share best practices.

The Information Technology Management Reform Act established a CIO Council to review and provide guidance on crosscutting information technology (IT) issues. During November 1996, the CIO Council designated the Year 2000 Interagency Committee as an official subcommittee and renamed it the CIO Council Subcommittee on Year 2000. The Subcommittee was instrumental in assisting OMB's development of the Y2K quarterly status report.

President's Y2K Conversion Council

Executive Order 13073 established the President's Council on Year 2000 Conversion in February 1998. The Council has the mandate to oversee agencies' activities to assure that their systems operate smoothly through Y2K. It is responsible for coordinating the federal government's Y2K efforts. Representatives from more than 30 major federal executive and regulatory agencies comprise the Council. These executive representatives are sufficiently senior so as to have 1) extensive knowledge of their agencies' Y2K efforts and external organizational relationships and 2) authority to commit their agencies.

The Council has established over 30 sector groups with coordinators from the appropriate federal agencies charged with outreach into the public and private sectors, both domestically and internationally. Looking internally at federal systems, the Council's oversight includes ensuring that adequate financial and personnel resources are committed to federal Y2K efforts and that they are used effectively.

Assessments

Cost estimates continue to be on the rise for federal agencies. Since August, estimates have risen $1 billion to $6.4 billion. Over 80% of the increase is attributable to three departments: Health and Human Services (HHS), Treasury, and Defense. HHS hiked its estimate $165 million for potential contingencies in fiscal year 2000, Treasury increased its estimate by $53 million for increased testing and validation and Defense jumped $591 million for increased independent verification and end-to-end testing. With much testing to go and schedules closer to possible slippage, it is likely that these cost estimates will continue to rise.

Sixty-one percent of federal mission-critical systems are now reported as compliant. This is a 10% increase since August. The remaining 39% is scheduled for completion by March 1999. Unfortunately, slippage is already apparent. Ten percent of mission-critical systems did not reach the renovation milestone of September 1998. As we move further into 1999, the risk of schedule slippage will increase.

Currently, of 24 major agencies that comprise the federal CIO Council, six are in Tier 1, seven in Tier 2 and 11 in Tier 3.

Tier	Agencies
One	DOD, DOE, HHS, DOS, DOT and AID
Two	USDA, DOC, Education, DOL, DOJ, Treasury and OPM
Three	DOL, VA, EPA, FEMA, GSA, HUD, NASA, NRC, NSF, SBA and SSA

Table 1: Current Status of Federal Agencies

Table 1 identifies these agencies by tier. This is based on self-reported progress on mission-critical systems.

Concerns

The Committee is very concerned about current agency progress. Despite an apparent increase in activity, it is still not enough. Many schedules show a steep improvement curve just before key OMB milestones. Both internal audit reporting and GAO reporting support the concern over schedule. Furthermore, hearings by the House specifically focused on the federal government's preparedness continue to raise warning flags. The federal government has never received a passing grade on any of the six report cards issued by Congressman Stephen Horn. Additionally, a large portion of testing, known to be one of the largest portions of the overall Y2K effort, is yet to come. Several agencies stand out as ones that require focused oversight and stepped up efforts due to the risks associated with their current pace of progress: Healthcare Finance Agency (HCFA), Federal Aviation Administration (FAA), Department of Energy (DOE) and Department of Defense (DOD). In light of these risks, these agencies' business continuity and contingency plans become even more important.

The area of system interfaces is another concern that requires additional attention. These interfaces exist internally within each federal agency; they exist between different agencies, between agencies and state governments, and between agencies and local governments. Generally, these interfaces support government revenue collection systems and benefits payment systems. Often, it is not clear who is responsible for interfaces among federal, state and local governments. Furthermore, the testing is complicated by the need to test these interfaces as a portion of the overall testing strategy.

One prime example is HCFA, which is one of the farthest behind in its critical systems remediation efforts. HCFA manages Medicare, Medicaid and Child Health programs serving over 74 million Americans. Problems with federal systems combined with Y2K failures in state and local government systems, or the interfaces between them, could result in delayed benefit payments, payments not being received at all or delivered to the wrong party, eligible recipients not receiving payments or incorrect amounts disbursed. Given the extreme volume of transactions that occur daily to support these programs, a contingency plan consisting of manual processes would not suffice.

Finally, half of the emergency supplemental funds for nondefense agencies have already been released within the past 2 months. These funds were intended to stretch over a 3-year period, which suggests that little will remain for true emergency requirements. It is not clear that OMB scrutinized funding requests as closely as the Committee would have hoped. While OMB is experienced in overseeing budgetary requests, another entity more involved with the Y2K issue, such as the President's Council, might have been better fit to evaluate the Y2K funding requests. Unfortunately, suggestions from the House to give more authority and responsibility to the President's Council have yet to take root.

Department of Defense

In addition to the concerns expressed above, the Department of Defense (DOD), as the largest federal agency with nearly half of the federal government's computer assets, faces a monumental management challenge in addressing Y2K. The department relies on computer systems to conduct nearly all of its functions, including strategic and tactical military operations; sophisticated weaponry; intelligence collection, analysis, and dissemination; security efforts; and more routine business operations such as payroll and logistics.

The breadth of the problem confronting DOD is enormous: it has more than 1.5 million computers, 28,000 automated information systems and 10,000 networks. Its information systems are linked by thousands of interfaces that exchange data within DOD and across organizational and international lines. Furthermore, DOD's reliance on computer systems is increasing as technology changes the traditional concepts of warfighting through improved intelligence and rapidly modernized command and control. Successful defense operations will depend greatly on the department's ability to ensure that its systems and the systems with which they interface are Year 2000 compliant.

According to the U.S. General Accounting Office (GAO), which published a series of reports last year on DOD's overall efforts to address the Year 2000 problem, the department's efforts pose considerable risks. DOD still does not have reliable, timely information on program status, because information being reported up-the-chain is not validated for accuracy or completeness. GAO found instances in which defense components' reports on systems compliance were often inaccurate. In addition, GAO found that guidance issued by the department to its components on issues such as interfaces, testing, and reporting has been inconsistent, leading to false starts and uncoordinated efforts. GAO also found that DOD's contingency plans, developed in the event of systems failures, are frequently not executable.

DOD's Inspector General and other internal audit offices have issued over 130 reports that similarly question the department's management of its Year 2000 program. These audit reports repeatedly revealed many of the same findings as those reported by the GAO, as well as problems experienced in assessing and inventorying systems, effectively determining and allocating resources, and accurately testing and certifying systems' Year 2000 compliance. The department's audit reports also revealed that much of DOD's base level infrastructure, such as security systems, telephone switches, traffic control systems, and water and sewage treatment systems are vulnerable to Year 2000 problems.

These findings and risks are reflected in the Office of Management and Budget's assessment of DOD as a "Tier 1" agency, i.e., an agency showing "insufficient evidence of adequate progress." DOD senior management has been responsive to the GAO and internal audit findings and has taken an active, highly visible interest in implementing corrective actions. The senior management team has improved its oversight of the Year 2000 program so that it can more effectively assess program direction and take actions based on this assessment and known problems. However, DOD remains behind schedule in completing its systems remediation and is at considerable risk of being unable to successfully meet the Year 2000 deadline.

State and Local Government

Overview

In addition to the 50 state governments, there are 3,068 county government jurisdictions and approximately 87,000 other local government jurisdictions within the United States.

These state, county, and local governments deliver the majority of the essential services upon which citizens rely each day. These include police, fire, and emergency medical services response; financial support networks, including welfare and Medicaid payments; unemployment insurance payment systems; disability claims; and basic utilities, such as water and wastewater, sanitation, and local transportation systems. While the prospect of preparing federal government systems is daunting, the challenge of assuring the Y2K preparedness of these other sectors of government is even more mammoth. The consequences of failures in this sector are as potentially grave to the public as failures in the vital sectors of power and telecommunications.

Major Initiatives

Several of the largest intergovernmental councils and professional organizations are actively engaged in Y2K awareness programs. The National League of Cities, the National Association of Counties, and the International City/County Management Association, in conjunction with Public Technology, Inc., are sponsoring a Y2K awareness program entitled "Y2K and You."

The Metropolitan Washington Council of Governments has published a Year 2000 Best Practice Manual. These programs are good examples of what an effective dialogue between state, county, and local governments can achieve.

In his testimony before the Committee on October 2, 1998, the Honorable Michael O. Leavitt, governor of Utah and vice chairman of the National Governor's Association (NGA), described several NGA initiatives aimed at assisting the states with Y2K preparation. In July 1998, the NGA held a "Year 2000 State Summit" which focused on state, local, and private-sector coordination and on establishing a common agenda to increase public confidence in state services. The NGA has also published an issue brief entitled "What Governors Need to Know About Y2K," which Governor Leavitt stated "outlines the steps governors should take as chief executive officers, guarantors of public safety, and public leaders." Both the State of Texas and the State of Pennsylvania have been recognized as having two of the most extensive and well-developed state Y2K programs. New York State Governor George Pataki has also been leading the call for Y2K preparedness in his state.

Assessments

The assessments of Y2K progress in the sector of state and local government are not optimistic.

The National Association of State Information Resource Executives (NASIRE) is conducting a continuing survey of individual state Y2K preparedness. The Gartner Group has also conducted a state government Y2K survey. The National Association of Counties (NACO) recently commissioned National Research, Inc. to conduct a random survey of the Y2K status of county governments. The General Accounting Office (GAO) is examining the status of federal to state data exchanges. These include the vital connections through which funding from the federal government is provided to the states for various aid programs.

Unemployment, for example, is federally funded, but state administered. The Department of Labor reported in December that the following states were behind in remediating their unemployment systems: Connecticut, Delaware, the District of Columbia, Hawaii, Illinois, Kansas, Louisiana, Massachusetts, Missouri, Montana, New Hampshire, New Mexico and Vermont.

In his testimony before the Committee on October 2, 1998, John Thomas Flynn, CIO of the State of California, and president of NASIRE stated that compliance among the 50 states with all aspects of mission-critical legacy systems ranged individually from under 10% complete, to more than 90% complete. According to the NASIRE survey results, just under half (24) of those responding had completed remediation of at least 50% of their mission-critical systems. Mr. Flynn noted that no state had declared itself 100% complete as yet.

Data provided by the Gartner Group indicate that only 50% of the states are evaluated as at Level III Status under the Gartner Group's scale. A Level III rating indicates that the state has completed its project plan; has assigned resources; has completed a detailed risk assessment, remediated; and has tested 20% of mission-critical systems, conducted vendor reviews and has completed contingency plans. Thirty percent of the states are listed at Level II, indicating that they at least have developed an inventory of operational dependencies. Ten percent of the states are evaluated as Level I, indicating that they have begun their projects, are aware of the problem, and have begun conducting their inventories. The remaining 10% are evaluated as "uncertain," indicating they were unaware of their Y2K preparedness status.

The GAO has advised that as of November 1998, 33 states had completed 75% of their verification of federal data exchanges. GAO found that as of June 30, 1998, approximately one half of the state disability determination systems had not been renovated, tested, and certified Y2K compliant. Additionally, over 90% of state Medicaid, 70% of state Temporary Assistance for Needy Families and 75% of the state Food Stamp Program systems were not Y2K compliant as of August 1998 according to GAO statistics.

Survey data recently released by NACO, collected from 500 counties, indicate that only 50% of the respondents have countywide plans to address Y2K issues. Of the 16 counties with populations over 500,000, all but one have a countywide plan. Seventy-four of the 119 counties having populations below 10,000 reported that they have not prepared a Y2K plan.

Fifty-four percent of the counties surveyed reported that they have no contingency plans for Y2K disruptions. Twenty-two percent reported that they had prepared Y2K contingency plans. Fifty percent of the largest counties in the survey stated that they have contingency plans, while only 19 of 119 counties in the smallest population group (population below 10,000)

Year 2000 Status of the 50 States

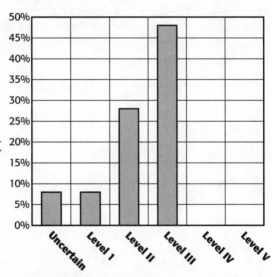

Note: *Data includes assessment of information systems owned and managed by state governments for purposes such as law enforcement, public health and education programs. It does not include private sector or county- and local-government computers or other infrastructures.*

Rating is done with GartnerGroup "COMPARE" methodology. Levels of readiness are defined as:

Level I Getting started, champion identified, awareness, begin inventory
Level II Develop detailed inventory of operational dependencies
Level III Project plan completed, resources assigned, detailed risk assessment, remediate and test 20% of mission-critical systems, vendor reviews, complete contingency plans
Level IV Complete remediation and testing of remaining 80% of mission-critical systems, contingency strategies implemented for mission-critical dependencies
Level V Remaining systems and dependencies completed and policies in place to avoid non-compliant issues after compliance is reached.

had one. The 500 survey respondents reported a total cost estimate of over $283 million for Y2K compliance.

A survey published by the Office of the New York State Comptroller in September 1998 indicates that 100% of New York's counties have made preparations for Y2K. Twenty-six percent of the cities, 54% of the towns, 48% of the villages and 61% of the fire districts reported that they had not made Y2K preparations.

Concerns
The Committee has serious concern about the Y2K readiness of state and local governments.

This concern is supported by all of the previously cited surveys, which, when taken, together indicate a vast disparity in the readiness level of the individual states, and a disturbingly low overall level of preparedness on the part of county and local government jurisdictions.

General Business

The general business sector portion of this report is organized into several sections. First, the small business to global corporations section serves to set the stage for business and Y2K in generic terms. The overview provides a look at the supply chain in general and highlights the interdependencies among links of the chain. Major initiatives within this section address activities of this Committee, an October committee hearing and a field hearing in Oregon; activities of the Manufacturing Extension Program; and United States Department of Agriculture (USDA) activities. In addition to the status information provided in discussion of the two Committee hearings, a separate section looks at two assessments of business. Finally, this section of the report focuses on several important industries not already addressed in the Committee's other seven sectors: pharmaceuticals, food and chemical manufacturing. Each of these industries has its obvious importance to the public's health, welfare, and well-being. The consequences to

> *"I believe that as businesses review their supply chains for Y2K preparedness we will see a 'flight to quality.'"*
>
> *Senator Bob Bennett*

the public of any one of these industries having significant disruptions due to Y2K is unacceptable. Therefore, "urgent" efforts for preparedness must increase.

Small Business to Global Corporations

Overview

As is the case with ever-increasing aspects of daily life, business has grown more dependent on technology—especially information technology. Not only has it changed our daily lives, it has changed our daily business. Competition in local, state, regional and international business markets has shrunk profit margins for all businesses—from small independent businesses to global conglomerates. Shrinking profit margins have motivated companies to reduce expense and increase efficiency. Information technology enables companies to regain a solid hold on profitability and stimulate growth.

American business has developed and adopted just-in-time inventory as the standard. Lean manufacturing is central to the success of most large, complex factory operations. Precision farming has led to increased production with fewer resources. The supply chain from raw material/basic ingredient production/provider, to preliminary processing, to manufacturer, to distributor, to wholesaler or retailer, and ultimately to final customer, has become ever tighter and shorter. The ripple effect from a problem at any point in this chain can be felt throughout the length of the chain. Information technology provides the backbone that fuses the chain at each link often via electronic commerce/electronic data interchange (EC/EDI).

Market and legal pressures continue to drive the majority of the decisions made within business, including Y2K decisions. A National Federation of Independent Business (NFIB) Y2K study correctly noted that "information describing the [Y2K] problem needs to address consequences of inaction if it is to stimulate action." Although this study provides an assessment of the preparedness of small business, there is no community-wide assessment of Y2K preparedness within overall business. However, as has been the case in previous Committee hearings, the larger companies that have adequate resources to address the issue are generally in a better position regarding their Y2K efforts than small- and medium-sized companies.

Although it may seem contrary to what one would normally think, a system that actually crashes due to a Y2K problem causes a better situation than one that does not. In the case of a crashed system, it is clear there is a problem and a system diagnosis can reveal the cause. Technicians can fix the problem and bring the system back on line.

If a system experiences a Y2K related problem but does not crash, the system may continue to operate with the problem going unnoticed. System users will likely continue to use the system trusting it is operating correctly and the data or calculations it yields are correct. By the time the problem is identified, data may have been corrupted, business processes incorrectly run, and so forth. The impact of a Y2K problem such as this may far outreach the offending system to those systems with which it interfaces. Interfaces provide a conduit where one system's errors could propagate through numerous others.

"We must get the attention of top management and recognize that this is not an IT problem . . . This is a management challenge that must be addressed by the highest CEO immediately."

Senator Bob Bennett,
June 2, 1998

Alan Arnold, a senior Ernst and Young manager, cites some personally observed examples of Y2K problems. He notes that orders did not process correctly, supply channels failed, accounting reports aged incorrectly and invoice systems billed incorrectly. Certainly payroll systems are date-sensitive as they perform trivial to complex salary-related calculations. These are only topical examples of the Y2K problem.

Major Initiatives

Northwest Year 2000 Summit

Key Oregon businesses and industries provided expert testimony on July 1, 1998, at the Northwest Year 2000 Summit held in Portland, Oregon. Senator Gordon Smith, a member of the Special Committee on the Year 2000 Technology Problem, initiated and presided over the event geared toward assessing the potential impact of Y2K on both small and big businesses. Additionally, Senator Smith focused on the question "What role, if any, should the federal government play with respect to Year 2000 technology issues?"

Following testimony from Integrated Measurement Systems, Intel Corporation, WRG Design Company, Providence Health System, and Bank of America, the audience actively participated. The audience consisted of individuals from the American Electronics Association, local business groups and the Tualatin Valley Economic Development Corporation.

The testimony emphasized the need to prioritize efforts to concentrate on those issues that are critical to human safety, defense, and well-being. This clearly was one of the Committee's first tasks as it established its eight sector areas: utilities, health services, telecommunications, transportation, finance, general government, general business and litigation (in priority order). Concerns about litigation were heard numerous times both in the context of limiting frivolous lawsuits and providing protection for statements made in good faith. Certainly, the latter was addressed when the Year 2000 Information and Readiness Disclosure Act became law on October 19.

Finally, the issue of compliance certification validity was

raised. This issue has yet to be resolved. However, the Committee continues to emphasize the need for audits as well as independent verification and validation as a crucial element of a sound Y2K program.

A Hearing–Small Businesses to Global Corporations: Will They Survive the Year 2000?

On October 7, 1998, the Special Committee on the Year 2000 Technology Problem held a hearing focusing on areas within the general business sector. As with previous sector hearings, the purpose of the hearing was to increase awareness and disseminate reliable preparedness information as well as facilitate and stimulate solutions. Committee work supports polls showing only a small percentage of the American population has even heard of Y2K. Awareness is a continual process that will extend up to and past January 1, 2000.

During the hearing, a reoccurring theme appeared throughout the examination of the supply chain, from global corporations to small- and medium-sized business. Witnesses talked about a move from high-risk vendors to lower risk vendors. Senator Bennett concluded, "as a result of Y2K, we are going to see significant shifts in where people go for materials, where people go for markets. It will produce some very challenging social problems all over the world. Those countries and companies that survive and thrive as a result of the long-range planning that they have done will be called upon to provide aid and assistance in those parts of the world where those challenges exist. I think the social impact of this is beyond anything we had previously thought it might be."

Witnesses at this hearing provided testimony that looked at the overall business community preparedness, both domestically and internationally, of small and large business, and used the pharmaceutical industry as a case study. Opening the hearing, a special witness highlighted the possible personal and dramatic nature of the Y2K problem. Laurene West shared her story and concerns to bring a human face to the Y2K problem.

West's personal testimony dramatically depicted the critical dependency that many Americans have on the pharmaceutical industry. Without a daily supply of medication and the coordinated efforts of healthcare providers, Ms. West will die due to the residual effects of a brain tumor and a postoperative infection. She has 34 years experience within healthcare: 20 as a registered nurse and, most recently, 14 years developing and implementing medical information systems. Her primary message was that many Americans would feel the impact of medication supply and distribution disruptions that are possible from Y2K. During her testimony, she explored issues related to stockpiling medication for those dependent upon regular drug doses.

Testimony from pharmaceutical representatives later in the hearing responded to Ms. West's supply chain issues. Richard Carbray, General Manager of Pleton's Pharmacy and Home Health Centers, noted that at the pharmacy level, it is possible to identify groups of patients through their systems to ensure plentiful and sufficient quantities of medication are on-hand for each particular group. At the same time, he cautioned that individuals getting an excess supply unnecessarily might cause the available supply to change drastically. Dr. Charles Popper, CIO of Merck & Co., echoed the caution noting that stockpiling an excess supply would likely cause more harm than good. Dr. Popper believes that a more focused approach will aid in understanding what steps are necessary to cover this situation. However, good data are necessary. The Vital Signs 2000 survey will facilitate identifying supply chain sensitivities and risks.

Despite tremendous progress in resolving Y2K problems throughout 1998, much work remains in the limited time available. Almost a quarter of all companies worldwide, regardless of size or industry, has yet to start any Y2K effort, according to testimony by Lou Marcoccio, Research Director for the Gartner

Group. While the heavily regulated insurance, investment services and banking industries are the most advanced in their efforts, the healthcare, oil, education, agriculture, farming, food processing and construction industries are lagging dangerously behind.

Closely tied to the issue of failures is a misunderstanding of the Y2K problem. Many mistakenly think that Y2K problems will only manifest themselves at the stroke of midnight on December 31, 1999. However, Y2K problems have been occurring over the years and will continue to increase in occurrence as we approach January 1, 2000. Furthermore, they will continue to arise at a diminishing rate in the months following January 2000.

Mr. Marcoccio ended his testimony focusing on specific risks to the United States, stating, "from a domestic perspective, the risks that we have identified or highlighted as being most important are the interruptions or failures due to interdependencies and interconnections, between companies and countries." From an international perspective, Gartner Group's research indicates key foreign government agencies will likely experience significant failures. This fact highlights the critical nature and risk exposure of the interrelationship between our government agencies and militaries.

Shifting the focus to small business, the Honorable Fred Hochberg, Deputy Administrator, Small Business Administration (SBA), testified that to some extent, all of the nation's 23.6 million small businesses may be affected by Y2K. Their exposure is due to their reliance on office automation—hardware, software or equipment with embedded chips—any of which may be non-Y2K compliant. To assist the nation's small businesses as they cope with Y2K, the SBA emphasizes a three-step program:

1) conduct a self-assessment to identify possible affected computer hardware and software in addition to any equipment using embedded chips,

2) take action immediately, and
3) stay informed about Y2K issues. Included in this process are efforts to assess the Y2K status of businesses' suppliers and distributors as well as contingency plan development.

Although it may be "too late to start early," it is not too late to start.

When questioned about the availability of loans for small businesses to initiate Y2K efforts, Mr. Hochberg noted that all of SBA's loan programs today are available for Y2K remediation work. Senator Gordon Smith concluded from further explanation, "there is really no reason people should not be doing this [taking action on Y2K] in small business."

The NFIB report, "Small Business and the Y2K Problem," sponsored by the Wells Fargo Bank, is discussed in the assessment section below. Later in this section, the Manufacturing Extension Program (MEP) Y2K tool kit is covered as a resource to small manufacturing businesses for Y2K information. Representatives of both the NFIB and MEP testified during the hearing.

National Y2K Action Week

The President's Council on Year 2000 Conversion designated October 19–23 as "National Y2K Action Week." While many large firms have grasped how a Y2K failure could severely affect their futures, smaller firms seem more focused on their immediate problems. Therefore, on October 19, the President's Council on Year 2000 Conversion and more than 100 private sector organizations launched "National Y2K Action Week." The goal was to motivate managers of small- and medium-sized companies to take the necessary steps to ensure that the technologies they and their business partners depend upon are Y2K ready. The program core consisted of hundreds of educational events hosted by federal government field offices. Participating entities included the following:

- SBA's 69 district offices, 935 small business development centers, 65 business information centers, 35 women's business information centers and 18 tribal business information centers;
- the Department of Commerce's 400 manufacturing extension partnership offices and 65 minority business development centers;
- USDA's 3,100 county extension offices;
- the Social Security Administration's 1,350 field offices; and
- the Department of Transportation's 120 field offices.

These offices helped managers assess their businesses' Y2K vulnerabilities, develop strategies for remediation and replacement work, find technical resources for addressing the problem and formulate contingency plans. To further address concerns of businesses, SBA has a small business answer desk, 1-800-827-5722, which provides personalized response and assistance.

Manufacturing Extension Program (MEP)–Conversion 2000

MEP is a ready resource for small- and medium-sized manufacturing businesses. As a non-profit program of the Department of Commerce's National Institute of Standards and Technology (NIST), MEP has over 400 centers located throughout the 50 states and Puerto Rico. There are some 2,000 MEP engineers available nationally through these centers and field offices. They work directly with area firms to provide tailored expertise and services. Specifically targeting Y2K, NIST and the national MEP office developed a Y2K tool kit that manufacturing businesses that desire assistance can use. Thus, they are a pre-positioned resource available to assist in completing a thorough Y2K assessment and in initiating an appropriate plan to remediate, test, and implement Y2K solutions.

The Y2K self-help tool, Conversion 2000, leads a small business through four phases of assessing and structuring a Y2K program. Phase I facilitates the internal inventory of hardware, software, and embedded systems. Next, in Phase II, a business criticality assessment is conducted and initial criticality in addition to confidence ratings are calculated. Phase III activities involve contingency planning. Finally, Phase IV covers remediation planning and management.

Although this Y2K tool does not solve the Y2K problem for a business, it puts a business well on the road to soundly addressing Y2K, providing a roadmap of sorts. Furthermore, documentation produced from the use of Conversion 2000 will assist in application processing for SBA fast track loans for Y2K.

Cooperative State Research, Education, and Extension Service (CSREES), USDA–Y2K Community Awareness Outreach

CSREES is designed to be an agent for change and an international research and education network. Part of CSREES' mission is to promote informed decision-making by producers, families, communities and other customers through partnerships with public and private sectors that maximizes limited resources' effectiveness. Included in CSREES are over 9,600 local extension agents working in 3,150 counties nationwide; farm safety education programs in all 50 states and Puerto Rico; as well as international education programs taught by over 200 extension professionals in 17 countries. As part of National Action Week, CSREES rolled out its recently developed Y2K Community Awareness Outreach Toolkits. Five thousand of these "toolkits" were distributed to all county extension offices, USDA Foreign Agriculture Service's Agricultural Attaches, State Agriculture Commissioners, National Agricultural Statistics Service State Directors, the Land-Grant University System, 1994 Tribal Colleges and the Hispanic Serving Institutions.

Each "toolkit" consists of fact sheets, a media and information plan, a press release template, public service announcements (both written and recorded), a general public brochure, talking points and frequently asked questions. The fact sheets include: "Creating a Year 2000 Computer Action Plan," "Is Your Computer Ready for Y2K," "Preparing for the Year 2000 Computer Challenge" and "The Y2K Problem and Embedded Systems."

During the kick-off of National Y2K Action Week, USDA Deputy Secretary Richard Rominger noted that a memorandum of understanding (MOU) between the Departments of Agriculture and Commerce had been signed. The MOU focused on the needs of small businesses and manufacturers. As an outcome, it is likely that CSREES' "Y2K Toolkit" may merge with MEP's Conversion 2000 to form a single, more comprehensive "toolkit."

> *"To stimulate action, you must first identify the consequences of inaction."*
>
> William Dennis

Assessments

National Federation of Independent Business (NFIB)

On May 26, 1998, William Dennis, Senior Research Fellow for NFIB, published the report *Small Business and the Y2K Problem*. One of the most telling findings of the report was that over 80% of American small businesses are potentially exposed to Y2K problems. In Dennis' October 7 testimony, he further described the general assessment of small business. "A fifth of them do not understand that there is a Y2K problem . . . They are not aware of it. A fifth of them are currently taking action. A fifth have not taken action but plan to take action, and two-fifths are aware of the problem but do not plan to take any action prior to the year 2000."

Approximately 330,000 small businesses that are computer dependent fall into this last two-fifths category. Dennis suggests that if they lose their computers or if their computers malfunction, it will result in a production or sales loss of 85%. They will be out of business, effectively, until they fix the problem.

Over 82% of small businesses have some level of direct Y2K exposure due to their reliance on information technology and automation. The large majority of them, 81%, indicate awareness of the exposure. However, only half have taken or plan to take action in response to the exposure. The lack of action apparently comes from 77% of small businesses not considering Y2K to be a serious problem.

Indirect exposures to Y2K are sometimes overlooked. Figure 1 identifies some of the sources of indirect exposure that small businesses face. These exposures result from electronic interaction with business partners. Seventy-five percent of small businesses deal electronically with partners and thus are exposed to possible Y2K impacts if their partners are not prepared for Y2K. Exposure due to electronic interactions with financial institutions is clearly the smallest of those sources identified in NFIB's report. This exposure is probably smaller yet, since, as an industry, financial institutions are generally considered to be out front in their Y2K efforts.

Medium-sized businesses may actually face the greatest over-

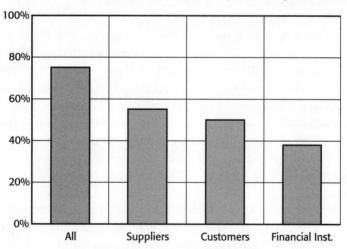

Figure 1: Source of Indirect Y2K Exposure

all Y2K exposure. Small businesses are likely to have less technology insertion within the business community. In many
cases, they may have the capability to go back to manual processing, if necessary. Even though small businesses generally
lack the resources to adequately address
Y2K issues, the impact of a failure is
likely to be moderate. Medium-sized
businesses, on the other hand, are more
likely to depend heavily on technology.
Manual processing may no longer present a viable option for medium-sized
businesses. They may also lack the
appropriate resources to remediate
affected systems and devices. Given that
small- and medium-sized businesses
provide over 51% of the private sector
output, the lack of action on their part may translate into a
larger ripple that moves through the closely linked supply
chain.

> *30–50% of all
> companies world-
> wide will
> experience at least
> one mission-
> critical failure.*

The NFIB report *Small Business and the Y2K Problem* is being
updated. Data collection is complete for the update and its
analysis is underway. The update should indicate the success of
National Y2K Action Week. The Gartner Group bases its
research and analysis on data gathered from 15,000 companies
in 87 countries. Data is updated every 90 days. The Gartner
Group's research has concluded that of all companies and government agencies, 23% have yet to begin any Y2K action. Of
these companies, 83% fall into the category of small companies.

Lou Marcoccio explained during the October 7 hearing that
"a mission-critical failure means that a business interruption is
likely to occur. It could affect revenue and will likely affect the
continued operation of that business." The Gartner Group predicts that 30% to 50% of all companies worldwide will experience at least one mission-critical failure. Within the United
States, that percentage drops to 15%. The typical amount of

time that one of these critical failures is expected to last is at least 3 days at a recovery cost of between $20,000 and $3,500,000 (this estimated cost does not include any costs related to possible litigation).

Figure 2 graphically portrays the number of companies expected to experience at least one mission-critical failure. Gartner predicts there is an 80% probability that these expectations are correct. The horizontal axis indicates the size of company and government agencies. The vertical axis indicates the percentage of all companies or government agencies of a particular size that are expected to experience at least one mission-critical failure. Shifting to looking at predicted mission-critical failures by industry sector, some logical conclusions can be drawn. Those industries that are most likely to have experienced a Y2K related problem earliest generally began to address the problem at that time. However, it is interesting to note that often they did not begin addressing the problem from a total business perspective. Frequently, only those areas of the business that experienced the failure or were most closely related to it were addressed. Heavily regulated industries also are gener-

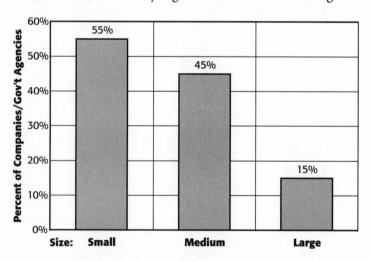

Figure 2: Predicted Mission-Critical Failures

ally in a better position with their Y2K efforts than those without regulation. Gartner's research covers companies and organizations across 27 industries. As with its predictions for mission-critical systems based on size (figure 2), it has developed failure predictions for companies within these 27 industries. To characterize these predictions, Gartner established four risk categories.

Each risk category, identified in the far-right column of figure 3, describes the percentage, in the far-left column of figure 3, of companies in industries within the category that will experience at least one mission-critical system failure. Taken alone, one mission-critical system failure does not sound like much. However, when you understand that thousands to hundreds of thousands of failures may occur either simultaneously or nearly simultaneously, the situation is much more serious.

Data provided by the Gartner Group and depicted in figure 3 clearly demonstrate that much work remains as we approach Y2K. For example, 50% of companies within the transportation industry will experience at least one mission-critical failure. Thus, the figure highlights those industries critical to our coun-

15%	Insurance, Investment Services, Banking, Pharmaceuticals, Computer Manufacturing	1
33%	Heavy Equipment, Aerospace, Medical Equipment, Software, Semiconductor, Telecom, Retail, Discrete Manufacturing, Publishing, Biotechnology, Consulting	2
50%	Chemical Processing, Transportation, Power, Natural Gas, Water, Oil, Law Practices, Medical Practices, Construction, Transportation, Pulp & Paper, Ocean Shipping, Hospitality, Broadcast News, Television, Law Enforcement	3
66%	Education, Healthcare, Government Agencies, Farming & Agriculture, Food Processing, Construction, City & Town Municipal Services	4

Figure 3: Failure Predictions by Industry

try's infrastructures that must continue to aggressively execute their Y2K plans as well as develop realistic and feasible contingency plans.

Concerns

In preparation for the October 7 hearing, the Committee staff conducted interviews with a variety of knowledgeable parties. Interviewees included federal agencies with purview over many aspects of business, especially those related to small business and the food industry; large businesses in manufacturing, distribution, and retail; and trade organizations representing a cross section of the business community.

International Business

All global corporations obviously have dependencies on other countries of the world, certainly to export their products, but also to import key supplies and raw materials for end products produced in the U.S. Examples of these dependencies are automobile parts from Southeast Asia, oil from Venezuela and insulin from Denmark. Y2K information is sparse, both on the international companies themselves as well as the infrastructure of the countries where they reside. The U.S. is purportedly the leader in Y2K remediation. This suggests that other countries are dangerously behind. Many have not even begun to address the problem. Thus, we should remain very skeptical about our ability to buy or sell goods from certain parts of the world.

With the main exception of the United Kingdom, the Netherlands and Scandinavia, European countries have taken a strikingly relaxed attitude to Y2K. A main-board director of a leading French bank said, "The year 2000 question is a conspiracy cooked up by the Americans and the British to create a smoke screen and distract attention away from preparations for the single European currency." The situation in Russia and China is even worse than in Europe.

Small and Medium Business (Fewer Than 500 Employees)

In a recent article by the president of NFIB, possible consequences for small- and medium-sized businesses were outlined: automatic funds transfers and direct deposits may be disrupted, fail, or occur at the wrong time; telephonic voice mail may fail; and fax machines may cease to properly transmit to and receive from customers. Mr. Dennis, the NFIB hearing witness, has stated that "more than 330,000 firms risk closing their doors until the problem is fixed, and more than 370,000 others could be temporarily crippled."

Another example of how critical Y2K preparation by small- and medium-sized businesses has become was published in a recent issue of the *CIO Communications, Inc.* publication. The example highlights the possible indirect consequence of failure to act. Sears Roebuck links 5,000 vendors into their EDI/telecommunications network. Of those, only 18% have been identified as critical to Sears' business processes. Thus, 82% of their current business partners—primarily small businesses—were deemed non-critical. As a triage approach to looking at work prioritization and resource allocation in addressing potential Y2K problems is necessary, this same approach is being applied by larger businesses as they assess Y2K related risk associated with their vendors. Once a vendor has not passed muster in this context, it is possible it will lose the business relationship permanently resulting in a devastating impact on its business.

Pharmaceuticals

While generally considered to be one of the leaders in the Y2K remediation effort, pharmaceuticals are caught in the classic squeeze of dependency on suppliers and distributors. Because of FDA regulations intended to protect the public, pharmaceutical companies must have a pre-approved ingredient supplier whose product is registered upon arrival for a particular drug product batch. This means that a constant supply source is critical to the drug manufacturing process. On the sales/distribution side, the companies sell 80% of their product through wholesale drug firms, thus requiring minimal direct sales. It is essential for success that both sides of the equation function effectively through this Y2K window of risk. The pharmaceutical companies are encouraging their colleagues in allied businesses to be Y2K prepared.

Food Industry

A $25 billion (U.S. $) international food retailer with chain stores in the U.S., Europe, Latin America, and Asia described a Y2K experiment that was conducted in one of its stores. It set the date for the store's computers to Y2K. The effect was "the computers shut down the store in 5 minutes. Everything was shut down. The security systems, the temperature controls, the safes, the front end. Everything."

The Food Marketing Institute published a Y2K white paper that further illustrated possible consequences of failure to act:

- ordering systems will ship the wrong products and incorrect quantities due to date errors in complex calculation routines,
- point-of-sale systems will have wrong prices because the host system selects the wrong item maintenance records,
- customers will be frustrated by frequent shopper systems that don't provide expected rewards due to failures in purchase history date calculations,
- credit cards will be rejected if their expiration dates are beyond Y2K,
- food manufacturers will label products with incorrectly calculated "sell by" dates, causing potential illness,
- pharmacy systems will cancel prescription benefits due to date problems and

- security systems will allow suspicious activity to continue due to date tracking errors.

Any interruption within the farm-to-fork chain can result in a direct loss to those who supply food, likely translating into food shortages and price increases. As is the case with many businesses, food suppliers are increasingly dependent on computerized processing and information exchange. For example, farmers and ranchers use electronic equipment irrigation systems, animal feed systems and transport systems. Processors rely on automated systems that help prepare and package consumer-ready products. Distributors, wholesalers and retailers depend on computer-driven equipment to transport, deliver, store, display and sell food products, and inventory and accounting systems. They rely further on equipment with time-dependent embedded computer chips, such as harvesting equipment; grain elevators; plant, warehouse and truck refrigeration systems; store and plant security systems; and heating, ventilation and air conditioning (HVAC) systems.

Committee efforts to coordinate interviews as well as to secure witnesses for hearings met significant resistance. This resistance and non-responsiveness came from both industry trade organizations/associations as well as major corporations within the retail and manufacturing sides of the food industry. Both food retailers and manufacturers cited numerous reasons for their resistance.

As of the 105th Congress, the general preparedness of the food industry is not clear. The reluctance to provide public witness is certainly disturbing. Put in the context of the Gartner Group's assessment of the food processing and farming/agriculture status, it is possibly alarming. Gartner predicts there is a better than 66% chance of at least one mission-critical failure within each of these industries (see figure 3). In testimony, Gartner's Marcoccio stated, "An industry highly overlooked is agriculture (farming, food processing, transportation/ distribution, and import and export of foods and food by-products). Several agriculture sub-industries are lagging far behind."

Chemical Manufacturing

Overview

Virtually every consumer product is critically dependent on the chemical manufacturing industry. Cars and trucks, for instance, depend on thousands of chemicals—from polyurethane seat cushions and neoprene hoses and belts to air bags and nylon seat belts.

Chemical manufacturing is also vital to the overall U.S. economy. In 1997, $69.5 billion in chemicals were exported, which was 10 cents of every export dollar. This topped agriculture's $55.9 billion of exports and aviation's $38.3 billion. In meeting the demands of the of U.S. industry, in 1997, the chemical industry shipped $392 billion of goods. This was 2.1% of the total U.S. economic output, more than any other manufacturing sector. Finally, over 1 million Americans were employed by the industry in 1997.

Y2K Vulnerabilities in Chemical Manufacturing

Chemical manufacturers are highly dependent on computers to manage businesses operations and to control manufacturing processes. Thus, they are susceptible to the Y2K problem as well. To quote from the Chemical Process Industries' (CPI) leading publication, *Chemical Engineering,* "Left unchecked, the Year 2000 problem—called Y2K, for short—could be catastrophic for the chemical process industries (CPI). The date glitch could cause innumerable shutdowns and horrific accidents. Indeed, a manufacturer's process-control system could be stymied by "00" and shut down altogether on New Year's Eve."

An example has already occurred. "At midnight on New Year's Eve 1996 at Tiwai Point in South Island, New Zealand, all [660] of the smelting potline process control computers

stopped working instantly, simultaneously, and without warning. The Bell Bay plant in Tasmania shut down two hours
later—midnight local time."

Major Initiatives

While the large companies have substantial ongoing Y2K programs, at this
time, the only major initiative across
the industry that the Committee is
aware of is a community workshop
convened at the Committee's request on
December 18, 1998. The committee has
requested that the United States Chemical Safety and Hazard Investigation
Board (CSB) investigate

> *"Those most at
> risk are small and
> medium sized
> companies."*
>
> Senator Gordon Smith

- the extent of the Y2K problem in the automation (both
  supervisory control systems and embedded systems) that
  monitors and controls the manufacture of toxic and hazardous chemicals;
- the awareness of large, medium and small companies
  within the industry of the Y2K threat;
- CPI progress to date in addressing the Y2K problem;
- the impact of this problem on the "Risk Management
  Plans" required in June 1999 under the Clean Air Act of
  1990;
- the role the Federal agencies are playing in preventing
  disasters due this problem; and
- actions to prevent major disasters due to toxic or hazardous chemical releases as the Y2K approaches.

Assessments

There are very few general Y2K assessments of the CPIs. The
Gartner Group provides one that surfaced in the Committee's

investigations. Gartner develops its predictions on Y2K from a quarterly survey of over 15,000 companies in 87 countries. It organizes its survey output into 26 industries, one of which is CPI. At the October 7, 1998, Hearing on General Business and the Year 2000 Problem, Lou Marcoccio of the Gartner Group placed CPI in Gartner's category III rating. In this category, Gartner predicts that about 50% of the companies will experience at least one Y2K mission-critical failure. Gartner's definition of a mission-critical failure is any business dependency, which, if it were to fail, would cause any of the following:

- a shutdown of business, production, or product delivery operations,
- health hazard to individuals,
- considerable revenue loss,
- a significant litigation expense or loss or
- significant loss of customers or revenue.

The Chemical Manufacturers Association (CMA) met with Committee staff following the October 7 hearing and related that they were prompted by Gartner's testimony to do their own, independent industry survey. Their survey has begun, but no results are available at this time.

Concerns

The Committee currently has two concerns about CPI. First is the potentially great public health risk posed by the accidental release of toxic or hazardous chemicals. The Committee is optimistic that from what it has learned, the very large CPI companies are well along in their Y2K preparations. However, as in other areas the Committee has looked into, small to medium firms are most likely unprepared. What's most bothersome here is that a small firm may be processing, transporting or storing enough dangerous chemicals to be a health or safety threat to a sizable population.

The second concern has to do with the publicly disclosed risk management plans required of firms in this industry in April 1999. These plans were required by the amended Clean Air Act of 1990 to provide citizens with accurate information about potential chemical hazards in their communities. These plans were initiated before the country was paying attention to the Y2K problem. The Committee feels that if Y2K is not considered as a potential cause of accidental release of chemicals that may be toxic or hazardous, these plans will not be credible or accepted by the public reviewing them.

In summary, the Committee is concerned that at this moment the impact of Y2K on chemical process safety may be a neglected issue. The Committee is hopeful that the President's Council on Year 2000 Conversion's assessments, the CSB-convened workshop in December 1998, and the Chemical Manufacturers Association survey will provide more assurance in the first quarter of 1999. The Committee will be watching these developments carefully and will be taking further action if more information is not forthcoming.

Litigation

The prospect of litigation arising from Y2K-related failures has been discussed since the Committee's first hearing. Both Chairman Bennett and Vice-Chairman Dodd recognized that the Y2K problem represents an attractive target for abusive lawsuits.

From the beginning, various sectors of industry told us they are hesitant to disclose and exchange information about their Y2K readiness—information that would help others in the remediation process—because they fear lawsuits if their disclosures prove inaccurate.

With the support of the White House, and in cooperation with the Senate's Judiciary Committee, Chairman Bennett and Vice-Chairman Dodd introduced S. 2392, the Year 2000 Information Readiness and Disclosure Act. The Act encourages the disclosure and exchange of information about the Year 2000 computer problem by limiting the liability of companies that provide good faith Y2K disclosure. S. 2392 was signed into law on October 19, 1998.

As the 105th Congress came to an end, it became clear that disclosure of Year 2000 readiness information is only one part of the problem. Many businesses are likely to have Y2K-related failures. Since our economic sectors are inextricably intertwined, one company's inability to fulfill its business contracts opens it and all the companies that depend upon it to liability. The result is a litigation domino effect, which allows the Y2K failure of one company to topple all of its business partners. A broad range of businesses and individuals will suffer some kind of economic injury, and many will undoubtedly seek recourse by filing lawsuits.

In 1999, the Committee plans to work together with the Senate's Judiciary and Commerce Committees in considering legislative proposals that would provide limited liability protection in Y2K-related matters. The Committee plans to hold hearings on the Y2K litigation issue in order to gather facts to assist the Congress in making any decisions on such legislative proposals.

International Preparedness

Assessing the Y2K preparedness of the international community has presented a special challenge to the Committee. While the Committee can call on federal regulators and industry representatives to report on the status of their respective areas, it is very difficult to get acceptable assessments from foreign countries.

The Committee has legitimate and compelling reasons to seek information regarding the status of its neighbors and trading partners. Besides the interdependent nature of the U.S. and world economy already emphasized in multiple sections of this report, the U.S. has a responsibility as a world leader to encourage a politically and economically stable environment.

Alerting countries to potential Y2K danger by encouraging the exchange of information is one way the U.S. fulfills this role.

Furthermore, the nation may be called upon to assist its neighbors in cases of severe Y2K impact. The U.S. has traditionally been one of the strongest supporters of humanitarian aid around the globe. It is unlikely that we will turn our back on the international community in the aftermath of Y2K. Therefore, the Committee advocates a proactive approach now so that Y2K-related repercussions are reduced later.

Overview

The Committee has tapped a number of sources for information on international Y2K preparedness. Within the government, agencies such as the State Department, Department of Commerce, Department of Defense, U.S. Information Agency and Central Intelligence Agency, have access to international information via their respective overseas operations. International organizations, such as the World Bank, United Nations and NATO, have provided varying degrees of insight. Finally, some private sector consultants have released reports rating the preparedness levels of certain countries.

The U.S. has a responsibility as a world leader to encourage a politically and economically stable environment.

With the exception of private sector consultants, most sources have hesitated to divulge specific information about foreign countries. The reasons for this are numerous. In many cases, the least prepared countries are those that depend heavily on foreign investment and multinational companies to supplement their economies. Panic over Y2K concerns may cause investors to withdraw financial support. Lack of confidence in a country's infrastructure could cause multinational companies to close their operations. The results could topple a fragile economy or a struggling foreign government.

Major Initiatives

The State Department recognizes the potential difficulties that embassies and foreign posts may face come January 1, 2000. As a result, the State Department sent a survey to 260 posts around the world, the results of which will be used to pinpoint troubled areas. The Y2K situations will be monitored throughout the duration of 1999, and, in cases of severe problems, the State Department will issue travel warnings, or encourage American nationals living abroad to return home. The State Department has already issued an edict stating that all embassies must be prepared to be self-sufficient for 30 days by January 1, 2000. More afflicted areas may necessitate longer-term plans.

In addition, the State Department chairs the International Relations Working Group of the President's Y2K Council. This working group plans to engage the U.S. embassies in Y2K assessments of their host countries and summarize results in a database that has been established by the U.S. Information Agency (USIA). Other federal agencies and the private sector are also expected to contribute to this assessment database, but the State Department is still working out a process for gathering and synthesizing all of this information.

The Department of Defense has concerns similar to those of the State Department, since many military personnel are stationed abroad and are dependent on their host countries' infrastructures. The Department of Defense, in conjunction with the State Department, is communicating with its foreign counterparts to raise awareness and generate international forums to address the Y2K problem. This includes such possible actions as inviting Russian and Chinese representatives to witness the millennium change from monitoring stations within the U.S.

The State Department Office of the Inspector General (OIG) is also engaged in Y2K assessments of selected countries. Countries covered to date include the following:

Latin America: Mexico, Chile and Panama;
Africa: South Africa, Gabon, Cameroon and Ethiopia;
Southeast Asia: Thailand, Hong Kong, Singapore and the Philippines.

The OIG has planned the following assessments for the upcoming months:

December: Mumbai and New Delhi, India;
January: Europe—Frankfurt, Bonn, Berlin, Rome, Paris, Athens, London, Moscow, Kiev and Warsaw; and

March: To be confirmed later, but may include China, Japan, Korea and Vietnam, as well as Bolivia, Paraguay and Brazil.

International organizations such as the World Bank and the United Nations have also engaged in Y2K outreach programs. From June through October, the World Bank conducted high-level national and regional seminars in developing countries. The World Bank is providing planning and implementation grants, as well as a tool kit for managing the Y2K problem. Besides issuing a June resolution encouraging international Y2K cooperation, the United Nations hosted a program in New York City with representatives from close to 100 countries on December 11, 1998. In order to encourage participation, as well as induce countries to appoint Y2K project managers, countries too poor to send a Y2K coordinator could receive World Bank funding for travel expenses.

Private sector consultants have used a range of data to speculate on the Y2K status of countries. Consultants often have special relationships with corporate clients, including access to proprietary data from multiple industries within a country. As a result, they can create models based on assumptions supported partially by hard numbers and partially by insider experience, and make fairly credible estimates. However, most consultants will not reveal specific client information, making model verification difficult. Additionally, even the most well-thought-out assumption can prove incorrect. In short, the Committee has interpreted forecasts with some skepticism.

Assessments

The Committee feels comfortable commenting on the preparedness of countries only in general terms. As a result, the Committee plans to focus its attention on international preparedness in the upcoming session.

Top-Tier Countries

At present, Canada, Australia, and the United Kingdom have consistently appeared on the top of preparedness lists.

Canada: In 1997, Canada established a government-industry task force to address Y2K issues across key sectors of the economy. Canada is encouraging compliance by providing small business tax relief for Y2K repairs. Additionally, a September Organization for Economic Cooperation and Development report stated that:

- 70% of businesses are taking action,
- 94% of medium and large firms are addressing the problem, and
- close to one-third of Canadian businesses indicate that their systems are ready.

Australia: Besides an internal Year 2000 Project Office, the Australian government established the Year 2000 National Strategy with $6 million (U.S. $) to alert private sector businesses to Y2K danger. Australia also took a strong position on Y2K disclosure for public companies, insisting on Y2K disclosure for all public Australian companies by June 30, 1998. As of July 1998, the following percentages of critical systems have been repaired:[1]

- 60% of underlying delivery of health and national services,
- 48% of social welfare and employment,
- 33% of revenue collection,
- 40% of national security (not including defense) and
- 34% of business critical functions in defense.

The United Kingdom: The U.K. has put considerable effort into convincing its European neighbors that the Y2K problem needs attention. In March of this year, Prime Minister Tony Blair stated that the U.K. was dedicated to bringing Y2K to the top of the international agenda. Besides conducting surveys through its embassies, the U.K. pledged $16.7 million (U.S. $) to the World Bank to support Y2K efforts in developing countries.

Even among the most Y2K conscientious countries, problems exist. Canadian Auditor General Denis Desautels submitted a report to his government on December 1, 1998. The report acknowledged improvement since a 1997 audit, but expressed concern that work still lagged in areas. As of June 1998, only four departments and agencies, responsible for 7 of the 48 mission-critical functions, had made "good" progress.

In Australia, PriceWaterhouse Coopers reported recently that while business and government Y2K spending had increased 47% in the past year, average expected project completion dates slipped from December 1998 to May 1999.

The U.K. also faces problems. Prime Minister Blair's attempt to raise an army of 30,000 "bugbusters" fell short by 29,900 bodies, as of a mid-September report. The low turnout throws doubt on the U.K.'s Action 2000 project's ability to galvanize the private sector.

This information on Canada's, Australia's and the U.K.'s Y2K programs cannot begin to represent the substantial efforts that these and other countries have made. Unfortunately, even countries that have received the best rankings still carry considerable Y2K risks, including the U.S.

Europe Overall

Cap Gemini, a consulting group with strong business relations throughout Europe and the U.S., conducts regular Y2K assessments of Norway, Finland, Denmark, Italy, Belgium, Sweden, France, the Netherlands, the U.K., Germany, the U.S. and Spain. Cap Gemini has taken the task of sizing the Y2K problem, using self-reported estimates of anticipated costs versus dollars spent. To compare countries of vastly different size, Cap Gemini reports data as percentages of annual information technology spending.

Cap Gemini's October data indicate that the U.S. still leads in remediation efforts as a percentage of estimated Y2K budget spent (61%). While the Committee is pleased to see this indication of progress, we recognize that dollars spent do not necessarily equate directly to completed work.

For example, Cap Gemini has expressed concern that some European countries have underestimated Y2K, and therefore have completed a smaller percentage of the necessary Y2K work than suggested by Cap Gemini's research.

The Committee is not convinced that American companies have not overestimated their preparedness as well. According to Cap Gemini, 5 out of 6 U.S. organizations express confidence in their business critical systems. Somewhat disturbingly, virtually all European countries express confidence in their systems. Fortunately, 98% of surveyed American companies are creating

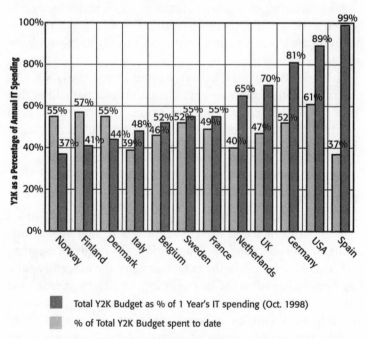

Total Y2K Budget as % of 1 Year's IT spending (Oct. 1998)

% of Total Y2K Budget spent to date

Cap Gemini's Y2K as a Percentage of IT Budget Estimated v. Spent

contingency plans, versus only 60% of European companies. These numbers do not, however, include companies with fewer than 100 employees.

Further bad news was released in December 1998 from the European Commission. The report warned member countries that efforts to bring systems in line with Y2K are not sufficient. The Commission also criticized the lack of information available about certain sectors and administrations, with the exception of the U.K.

Worldwide Comparison

Data become increasingly speculative outside of the previously discussed countries. Forecasts leverage such techniques as estimating computing personnel within a given country, projecting a country's volume of Y2K repairs based on the make-up of a given country's economy and estimating preparedness levels through in-country interviews, surveys and personal contacts.

It is a sophisticated and time-consuming process that results in imprecise data, at best. However, the Committee feels that even imperfect data provide more benefit now than perfect data 12 months from today.

Using such techniques, Dr. Howard Rubin, Chair of the Computer Science Department at Hunter College and Research Fellow for the Meta Group, has put together a table that provides an indicator of Y2K progress. The Robbins/Rubin Y2K Schedule Indicator quantifies the current level of progress versus the projected state of progress. A score of 1.00 indicates that a country's Y2K progress is on schedule. A value over 1.00 indicates that a country is ahead of schedule and a value of less than 1.00 indicates that a country is behind schedule. By Dr. Rubin's calculations, no country is ahead of or on schedule. The U.S. score, 0.87, still indicates that the U.S. is 13% behind schedule. On average, the countries included in this study scored 0.82, indicating that they have made 82% of their projected progress in addressing the problem. According to Dr. Rubin, 0.75 is an important cutoff score—after a project falls 25% or more behind schedule, it becomes virtually impossible to bring it back on schedule.

The Robbins/Rubin Indicator supports the Committee's sense that the U.S., the U.K., and Canada are in relatively good shape to face the millennium. Results from other countries are more surprising, especially when compared to the results of the Gartner Group's research.

The Gartner Group leverages its worldwide business network to collect information from 87 countries and 15,000 companies. In the Gartner Group's third quarter estimates, countries that

Country	Estimated Y2K Software Repair Cost	Estimated Y2K Total Repair Cost (% 1996 GDP)	Percent of Systems "Work in Progress"	Robbins/ Rubin Y2K Schedule Indicator
The USA	$187,921,430,000	2.5%	0.83	0.87
Sweden	$6,191,702,000	2.5%	0.78	0.86
The UK	$42,931,317,000	3.7%	0.82	0.85
Canada	$18,129,243,000	3.1%	0.81	0.85
Japan	$105,964,254,000	2.3%	0.78	0.85
France	$42,379,656,000	2.8%	0.78	0.84
Germany	$60,544,165,000	2.5%	0.79	0.84
Belgium	$7,232,049,000	2.7%	0.78	0.84
India	$4,037,957,000	1.2%	0.75	0.84
Russia	$32,246,348,750	7.3%	0.58	0.83
Netherlands	$10,199,431,000	2.6%	0.77	0.83
Austria	$9,894,632,000	2.5%	0.73	0.81
Italy	$33,731,929,000	2.8%	0.77	0.79
Portugal	$4,899,455,000	4.9%	0.69	0.79
Argentina	$8,292,548,000	2.8%	0.58	0.79
China	$4,442,256,500	0.5%	0.55	0.78
Korea	$22,614,322,500	4.7%	0.68	0.78
Brazil	$35,832,775,000	4.8%	0.61	0.78
Spain	$17,328,201,000	3.0%	0.72	0.77
Mexico	$19,250,198,000	5.7%	0.62	0.76
Average	$33,703,193,508	3.3%	0.72	0.82
Total	**$674,063,870,150**			

ranked in the top of Gartner's four tiers will see at least one mission-critical failure in 15% of all companies and government agencies. Third- and fourth-tier countries are predicted to see over 50% of their systems experience some level of interruption.

Comparing Results

Japan: While scoring a respectable 0.85 on the Robbins/Rubin Indicator, Japan has placed far lower on other rankings, such as the Gartner Group rankings.

Despite significant improvement in the past year, Japan may have underestimated the scope of the Y2K problem. According to a Bank of Japan survey, the majority of Japanese banks have neither engaged in contingency planning, nor checked the Y2K exposure of customers and counterparties. Since banking has proved to be one of the most aggressive sectors in addressing the Y2K problem around the globe, underestimation on the part of the Japanese banking sector may indicate even less awareness in other sectors.

France and Germany: France and Germany share a relatively high 0.84 Robbins/Rubin rating, and both received praise in the Cap Gemini report for significant improvement over the past 6 months.

However, qualitative reports suggest that France and Germany have yet to espouse a risk management approach to Y2K. The Committee feels strongly that Y2K is not just a technology problem, and worries that countries that simply focus on fixing the problem will fail to assess Y2K in a broad enough scope, and may fail to engage in contingency planning.

France and Germany may also suffer from a preoccupation with the conversion to the euro. In spring 1998, a survey by Neaman Bond, a consulting group, reported that both French and German companies ranked the euro conversion as more important than Y2K preparations. As two of the most ardent supporters of a unified currency, France and Germany may have

Gartner Group Predictions of Failure for Countries

15%	Australia, Belgium, Bermuda, Canada, Denmark, Ireland, Israel, the Netherlands, Sweden, Switzerland, the U.K., and the U.S.A.	1
33%	Brazil, Chile, Finland, France, Hungary, Italy, Mexico, New Zealand, Norway, Peru, Portugal, Singapore, South Korea, Spain, and Taiwan	2
50%	Argentina, Armenia, Austria, Bulgaria, Columbia, Czech Republic, Egypt, Germany, Guatemala, India, Japan, Jordan, Kenya, Kuwait, Malaysia, North Korea, Poland, Puerto Rico, Saudi Arabia, South Africa, Sri Lanka, Turkey, U.A.E., Venezuela, Yugoslavia	3
66%	Afghanistan, Bahrain, Bangladesh, Cambodia, Chad, China, Costa Rica, Ecuador, El Salvador, Ethiopia, Fiji, Indonesia, Laos, Lithuania, Morocco, Mozambique, Nepal, Nigeria, Pakistan, Philippines, Romania, Russia, Somalia, Sudan, Thailand, Uruguay, Vietnam, Zaire, and Zimbabwe	4

Note: Countries listed in alphabetical order

led the way in euro conversion at the expense of Y2K remediation.

Spain: Spain is behind in its Y2K remediation as indicated by all three research reports. Worth noting, however, is the pattern Spain's Y2K efforts seem to be taking.

Between April and October 1998, the percentage of Spain's estimated Y2K budget jumped from 22% to 99%, indicating a dramatic increase in awareness among surveyed institutions. Cap Gemini explained this tremendous change in terms of human nature. Companies are inclined to panic and overestimate expenditures when first faced with the scope of the Y2K problem. As Y2K projects organize themselves, estimates tend to fall as managers realize that a focused approach can save time and money.

This phenomenon highlights the importance of managerial guidance. While a technology department can fix a Y2K problem, it usually cannot make decisions about work prioritization, end-to-end testing and contingency planning without support from high-level management. Spain's massive jump in anticipated spending suggests that Spanish managers may have just discovered the Y2K problem and have yet to consider time- and resource-saving options, such as triage and contingency planning.

Concerns

According to Gartner, the majority of disruptions will be minimal. Only 10% of failures are expected to last more than 3 days. The question then becomes, which areas will face disruptions longer than 3 days and how severe will the impact of these failures be? This is the overall question that the Committee hopes to address in the following months.

Specifically relating to the international sector, the Committee has a special concern for the status of critical U.S. trading partners. The top trading partner of the U.S., Canada, accounts for 20.5% of the U.S. world trade (imports and exports). Japan accounts for 12% and Mexico 10.1%. While Canada falls in Gartner's top tier, Japan and Mexico are in the second and third tiers, respectively.

The Committee would also like to investigate the availability of critical imports, such as oil, in the light of potential Y2K disruptions. For example, the largest supplier of imported oil to the U.S. is Venezuela, which Gartner reports as 9 to 15 months behind the U.S. in its Y2K preparation. The Committee plans to seek more information on critical imports and trading partners.

As information on the impact of Y2K on the international front becomes more substantial, the Committee may consider the need to recommend certain governmental actions, such as targeted outreach programs, or post-Y2K recovery efforts. However, the Committee cannot know the direction that its involvement will take until it examines the international sector more closely.

Legislative Activities

S. 22, Commission on the Year 2000 Computer Problem Act
(Introduced September 1996)

This bill was the first legislative attempt to address the Y2K problem. It called for the establishment of a commission to study the Y2K problem and report the results to the President. The study would propose procedures for addressing federal, state and local government computer systems, as well as recommend levels of appropriation for remediation efforts.

S. 1518, The Year 2000 Computer Remediation
and Shareholder (CRASH) Protection Act of 1997
(Introduced on November 10, 1997)

The bill sought to require publicly traded companies to disclose five categories of information related to their Y2K remediation and risk management status without regard to materiality. The introduction of this legislation prompted the Securities and Exchange Commission to publish Staff Legal Bulletin No. 5 (January 12, 1998), a reminder to public operating companies, investment advisers and investment companies to consider their disclosure obligations relating to anticipated costs, problems and uncertainties associated with the Y2K issue. The staff legal bulletin was later superceded by Interpretive Release No. 33-7558, an enforceable, Commission-level release published on August 4, 1998.

S. 1671, The Examination Parity and Year 2000 Readiness for Financial Institutions Act (Introduced on February 24, 1998)

The legislation gave the Office of Thrift Supervision and the National Credit Union Administration (NCUA) explicit authority to examine and service corporations and subsidiaries owned by the insured institutions to the same extent that other financial institution regulatory agencies were permitted to do so. The legislation also required NCUA to take certain actions to enhance remediation efforts within the credit union sector. The Committee staff has already seen the positive results of this legislation, as regulators judiciously use the threat of cease and desist orders to keep financial institutions from doing business with unsound software contractors.

S. 2000, A bill to ensure that businesses, financial markets and the Federal Government are taking adequate steps to resolve the Year 2000 computer problem (Introduced on April 29, 1998)

In introducing this legislation, Chairman Bennett sought to amend the Employee Retirement Income Security Act of 1974 (ERISA) to require fiduciaries of employee benefit plans to consider the Y2K computer problem in making investment decisions. The legislation also would have codified the creation of the President's Council on Y2K Conversion. The Chairman felt that it was critical for the administration to dedicate more than a task force to this complex job. He wants the council to be vested with actual power, authority, and accountability.

S.2392, Year 2000 Information Readiness and Disclosure Act
(Introduced July 30, 1998)

Chairman Bennett intended to encourage the disclosure and exchange of information about the Y2K computer problem by limiting the liability of companies that provide good faith Y2K disclosure. S.2392 passed the Senate (amended) on September 28, 1998, and was signed into law October 19, 1998 (P.L. 105271).

Specifically, in all civil litigation including certain antitrust actions, the act limits the extent to which Y2K statements can be the basis for liability. It also prevents certain evidentiary uses, against the maker, of a subset of such statements. However, the act ensures that only responsible, good faith information-sharing receives such protection.

Committee Priorities for 1999

For the remainder of 1999, the Committee will continue to focus primarily on the seven industries addressed by this report. A renewed focus will be brought to bear on the crosscutting effects of increased litigation and the overall health of the world economy.

The Y2K problem is a dynamic one, and predicting with any certainty which new issues may arise is impossible. Nevertheless, there are certain areas that will be a high priority for the Committee in 1999. These areas include:

- Revisiting the domestic industry and infrastructure sectors first examined in 1998;
- Placing increased emphasis on international Y2K preparedness;
- Monitoring federal government preparedness, but turning more attention to state and local government preparedness;
- Evaluating contingency and emergency preparedness planning;
- Determining the need for additional Y2K legislation, or delaying implementation dates of new regulations;

- Examining litigation issues surrounding the Y2K problem; and
- Identifying national and international security issues and concerns.

Sector-Based Issues

In 1998, the Committee focused primarily on domestic Y2K issues. The Committee investigated critical infrastructure and industry sectors—utilities, healthcare, telecommunications, transportation, financial institutions, government and business—in an attempt to assess the Y2K status of each. Broad-based assessments were practically non-existent, making fact-based conclusions impossible. In that regard, Chairman Bennett's words seem even more appropriate: "We are flying blind into the Year 2000."

Additional information requested by the Committee on the status of various national and international industries is expected to be available in early 1999. The Committee will, therefore, continue its investigations and conduct hearings in each of these sectors throughout the first half of 1999.

Rather than a mere continuation of the broad-based hearings conducted in 1998, future hearings will be smaller and will focus on specific problem areas or industries in a given sector.

International Issues

Even if the U.S. could remediate all of its systems and embedded processors in time (which it cannot), it would, in an economic sense, still be at the mercy of the rest of the world.

The U.S. is part of, and dependent on, the global economy. Like the suppliers and partners within any given industry supply chain, America's vulnerability to the Y2K problem extends to other countries. The Committee's research into each infrastructure and industry sector highlights U.S. dependence on other countries, from Venezuela for oil to Denmark for insulin.

The Committee will turn its attention to countries economically and politically important to the United States. It will examine various sources of information to determine the state of readiness of these countries and if warranted, will recommend actions to assist in their remediation efforts or to reduce the risks unprepared countries pose to the United States.

Government Preparedness

The federal government openly shares information on its own Y2K preparedness. While not all of the findings are good, at least the information is available. Less visible is the status of preparedness of state and local governments. Their status of readiness will directly affect most Americans, because this is where they will turn if there is a failure in basic services, such as utilities.

The Committee is concerned that many state and local governments are not doing enough, either because they are unaware of their vulnerabilities or because they have insufficient resources. The Committee will continue to examine these issues in greater detail in 1999, and work with individual House and Senate members to take corrective actions where needed.

Contingency Planning

The Committee will continue to monitor the Y2K status of critical industry and infrastructure sectors, but will turn its attention to contingency and emergency preparedness planning in the last half of 1999.

The Committee will conduct hearings and make recommendations based on the results of its industry and infrastructure assessments conducted in the first half of the year. The Committee's goal will be to ensure the availability of basic emergency services and active contingency plans in the event of Y2K disruptions.

Legislation

The Committee will continue to examine the need for legislation or modifications to existing statutes and regulations. The intent of such legislation must be to provide incentive for greater remediation efforts, to ensure scarce resources are devoted to remediation, and to encourage both greater sharing of information and a fair approach to the litigation that might arise from Y2K problems.

Litigation

The Committee will continue to monitor and hold hearings on Y2K litigation issues. It will support efforts to minimize the impact of Y2K litigation on the court system while continuing to hold individuals and companies responsible for their actions.

National Security

The Y2K computer problem could pose a risk to our national security if not properly addressed. Broad issues such as the status of nuclear, chemical, and biological weapons and our ability to protect U.S. personnel and interests here and abroad are of utmost concern to all Americans.

The Department of Defense has monumental Y2K problems, and it is severely behind in addressing them. It is at risk of not completing remediation of all of its mission-critical systems in time. In addition, its infrastructure of more than 550 bases around the world may not be ready. For these reasons, the Committee intends to foster continuous and considerable attention on national security issues during 1999.

Appendix I: Recent Events

Several key events have occurred since the close of the 105th Congress. The following is a partial list.

President's Year 2000 Council

- On January 7, 1999, the President's Council on Year 2000 Conversion released its first quarterly summary of assessment information from its numerous industry-sector working groups. This report almost exclusively described the coordination processes at work in the various sectors and revealed little quantitative information on Y2K readiness.

Utilities

- On January 11, 1999, the North American Electric Reliability Council (NERC) issued its second quarterly report (fourth quarter 1998) to the Department of Energy. It boasted a 98% participation rate in its survey and reported steady progress in Y2K remediation. However,

56% of the nation's 3,200 electric utilities have yet to complete the most difficult phase of remediation and testing with less than 5 months to go to NERC's self-imposed deadline of June 30, 1999. The report indicates that several utilities will not make this deadline, including one-third of the nuclear power-generation facilities.

Healthcare

- The stockpiling of medications to ensure that 26.5 million chronically ill citizens are protected during the Y2K period remains an open issue. The Special Committee's Vice Chairman, Senator Christopher Dodd, has requested that the President's Council on the Year 2000 develop a policy and procedural solution by May 1, 1999.

Telecommunications

- On January 14, 1999, the Network Reliability and Interoperability Council presented its initial findings on the remediation efforts of the telecommunications industry which revealed that the industry plans to be Y2K ready by June 1999.
- The Teleco Forum completed its network testing and plans to release its report in February 1999. The Forum found no major interoperability problems in the network configurations tested. This testing focused heavily on the networks providing local phone service.
- The Alliance for Telecommunications Industry Solutions (ATIS) began testing for inter-network interoperability with results expected by the end of the first quarter of 1999. This testing will focus primarily on long distance phone service. ATIS will also be testing the Government's Emergency Phone System.
- In January 1999, the Joint Telecommunications Resources

Board (JTRB), which advises the President on emergency telecommunications allocations, met to discuss what role it would play in a Y2K emergency. This was the first meeting of the JTRB during the Clinton administration.

Transportation

- The December 1998 U.N. meeting of Y2K leaders from over 100 countries identified ports and maritime shipping operations around the world as an area of great concern. There is very little known about the Y2K readiness of this sector, which greatly influences the global economy. In the U.S., over 95% of imports and exports go through U.S. ports. To raise the visibility of the seriousness of this issue worldwide, the International Maritime Organization, a U.N. affiliate, will host a major conference and workshop on this topic in London during March 1999.

- The American Public Transport Association, the major trade association of American mass transit organizations, convened a Y2K workshop in Houston in January 1999. Over 100 organizations were represented. However, this was a small percent of the over 6,000 mass transit organizations in the U.S. Frank presentations at this meeting revealed that major metropolitan transit operations were not going to be completely ready for January 1, 2000. Contingency Planning and Continuity of Business Plans are a must for many entities in this sector if major disruptions in public transit systems are to be avoided in the early part of 2000.

Financial Services

- The results of third quarter SEC filings of public companies were mixed. While a far larger percentage of public

companies addressed Y2K in their filings, many disclosures revealed little in the way of significant information.

General Government

- The United States Fire Administration is currently conducting a survey of 4,300 Public Safety Answering Points
  to assess the readiness of 911 Systems nationwide. Less
  than ten percent of those surveyed have responded to
  date, and no firm conclusions can be reached about the
  data at this point.
- FEMA has commenced the first of a series of ten regional
  Y2K Preparation and Consequence Management Workshops. These workshops are intended to provide a forum
  where emergency management and fire services communities can discuss initial Y2K compliance assessments,
  potential consequences of Y2K disruptions, and coordination of local, state and federal responses. These workshops are in preparation for the national-level Y2K
  consequence management exercise scheduled in Washington, D.C., in June 1999.
- FEMA made significant strides in preparing the nation's
  emergency services by initiating the process to amend
  the national Federal Response Plan to account for potential Y2K disruptions and events. This plan coordinates
  the Federal government's response to major emergencies
  and disasters. FEMA also initiated a series of regional
  contingency planning meetings in February to coordinate Federal and local Y2K preparations.

General Business

- In December 1998, the Food Supply Working Group,
  chaired by the US Department of Agriculture, of the
  President's Council on Y2K Conversion released an ini-

tial assessment of Y2K and the food supply. The assessment covered three areas: domestic food supply; imports and exports; and transportation. The report said, "the state of readiness within the food industry is encouraging. An interruption in the food supply so severe as to threaten the well-being and basic comfort of the American public is unlikely." The assessment is based on a December 11, 1998, report by the Gartner Group on behalf of USDA.

- The National Federation of Independent Businesses, released the report, "Small Business and the Y2K Problem, Part II," on January 5, 1999. It concludes that for most small business owners Y2K is not a priority. For those that have taken action to address Y2K, the cost has been minimal.

- On December 16, 1998, Food Distributors International (FDI) completed their second survey intended to measure their members' Y2K readiness. Both surveys indicated that all respondents had a Y2K compliance program. However, the second survey highlighted two areas of concern: late Y2K program target completion dates and the lack of plans to perform business continuity or contingency planning. FDI plans to repeat this survey at six-week intervals.

- On February 5, 1999, the Senate Special Committee on the Year 2000 Technology Problem held its first hearing of the 106th Congress. This was the first of two hearings focusing on the Y2K preparedness of the food supply— from "farm-to-fork." Senator Richard Lugar, Chairman of the Senate Agriculture, Nutrition, and Forestry Committee; The Honorable Daniel Glickman, Secretary of the Department of Agriculture; Tyrone Thayer, Corporate VP & President of Cargill Foods; Allen Dickason, CIO of Suiza Foods Corp.; and Ken Evans, President of the Arizona Farm Bureau provided expert testimony at the hearing. Testimony indicated significant progress has been made since October 1998 within the United States food supply chain. However, it also showed that there is much remaining to be done in the remaining months of 1999. The second hearing is scheduled for March 2, 1999, and will include witnesses from SUPERVALU, Kroger, Kraft, Nestle, the Food Marketing Institute, and Grocery Manufacturers of America.

- On February 17, 1999, FDI released the results of their third Y2K member survey. As with the previous two surveys, both late Y2K program target completion dates and the lack of plans to perform business continuity or contingency planning are a concern. However, the responses did indicate increased confidence in respondent's ability to meet their own internal Y2K goals.

International

- On December 11, 1998, the United Nations sponsored a daylong international Y2K event. Over 120 member nations sent representatives. For many nations, this represented an opportunity for coordination with their neighbors and trading partners. Unfortunately, for others, it marked the beginning of their countries' Y2K remediation efforts.
- On January 26, 1999, the World Bank released the results of its survey of 139 developing countries. Only 54 countries had initiated national Y2K programs, and just 21 were taking concrete steps to remediate their computing systems. The World Bank concluded that developing countries face serious hurdles in addressing their Y2K problems, including lack of awareness, funding, and available IT professionals.
- A survey by Taiwan's Y2K office indicated that 40% of one million small- and medium-sized businesses have taken no action to remediate their computer systems.

Pending Legislation

- S. 96—The Y2K Act (Introduced January 19, 1999)

The bill intends to regulate interstate commerce by providing for the orderly resolution of disputes arising out of Y2K-based problems. Among other things, the bill provides that a Y2K action may not proceed to trial unless the defendant has been given the opportunity to fix the problem; imposes a cap on punitive damages; and sets forth liability rules that apply to product sellers, renters, and lessors.

- S. 174—The Y2K State and Local Government Assistance Programs (GAP) Act of 1999 (Introduced January 19, 1999)

The bill provides funding for states, through grants, to help states and local governments make programs they administer Y2K compliant. Grant applications must describe a proposed plan for the development and implementation of an applicable Y2K compliance program, along with a proposed budget, a request for a specific funding amount, and an identification of a funding source for completion of the plan if applicable.

- S. 314—The Small Business Year 2000 Readiness Act (Introduced January 27, 1999)

The bill establishes a program under which the government, through the Small Business Administration, will guarantee loans made to small businesses to remediate their Y2K problems and to provide relief for a substantial economic injury incurred by the small business as a direct result of Y2K problems.

- H.R. 179 The Businesses Undergoing the Glitch (BUG) Act (Introduced January 6, 1999)

The bill provides a tax deduction from gross income for the Year 2000 computer conversion costs of small businesses.

The aggregate amount allowed as a deduction is limited to $40,000.

- H.R. 192—The Year 2000 Consumer Protection Plan Act of 1999 (Introduced January 6, 1999)

The bill provides judicial and administrative proceedings for the resolution of Year 2000 processing failures. Among other things, the bill requires the clerk of the court receiving a Y2K-related complaint to refer that complaint to a mandatory arbitration proceeding, sets forth a standard of proof for recovering damages for Y2K-related failures, and places a cap on punitive damages.

Appendix II:
Acronyms Used in This Report

AGA	American Gas Association
AHA	American Hospital Association
AMA	American Medical Association
AMSA	Association of Metropolitan Sewerage Agencies
AMWA	Association of Metropolitan Water Agencies
AOPL	Association of Oil Pipelines
APCO	Association of Public Safety Communications Officials
APGA	American Public Gas Association
APPA	American Public Power Association
APTA	American Public Transit Association
ATA	Air Transportation Association
ATC	Air Traffic Control
ATIS	Alliance for Telecommunications Industry Solutions
ATS	Air Traffic System
AWWA	American Water Works Association
BCAG	Boeing Commercial Aircraft Group
CAD	Computer Aided Dispatch
CEA	Canadian Electric Association

CEO	Chief Executive Officer
CIO	Chief Information Officer
CMA	Chemical Manufacturers Association
COTS	Commercial Off-The-Shelf Software
CPE	Customer Premise Equipment
CPI	Chemical Process Industries
CRASH	Computer Remediation and Shareholder
CSB	Chemical Safety and Hazard Investigation Board
CSREES	Cooperative State Research, Education, Extension Office
DCS	Digital Control System
DOC	Department of Commerce
DOE	Department of Energy
DOJ	Department of Justice
EC	Electronic Commerce
EDI	Electronic Data Interchange
EEI	Edison Electric Institute
EMS	Emergency Medical Services
EPA	Environmental Protection Agency
EPRI	Electric Power Research Institute
ERISA	Employee Retirement Income Security Act
FAA	Federal Aviation Administration
FCC	Federal Communications Commission
FDA	Food and Drug Administration
FDIC	Federal Deposit Insurance Corporation
FERC	Federal Energy Regulatory Commission
FFIEC	Federal Financial Institutions Examination Council
FRB	Federal Reserve Board
GAO	General Accounting Office
GETS	Government Energy Telecommunications System
GISB	Gas Industries Standard Board
GPA	Gas Processors Association

GRI	Gas Research Institute
GSA	Government Service Administration
HCFA	Healthcare Finance Agency
HF	High Frequency
HIMA	Health Industry Manufacturers Association
HUD	Housing and Urban Development
HVAC	Heating, Ventilation and Air Conditioning
IATA	International Air Transport Association
ICAO	International Civil Aviation Organization
ICI	Investment Company Institute
INGAA	Interstate Natural Gas Association of America
IPAA	Independent Petroleum Association of America
IT	Information Technology
ITAA	Information Technology Association of America
ITU	International Telecommunications Union
JCAHO	Joint Commission Accreditation of Healthcare Association
JIT	Just in time
LANs	Local Area Networks
LNP	Local Number Portability
MEP	Manufacturing Extension Program
MOU	Memorandum of Understanding
MTA	Mass Transit Agencies
NACO	National Association of Countries
NAS	National Airspace System
NASA	National Air and Space Administration
NASIRE	National Association of State Information Resource Executives
NATCA	National Air Traffic Controllers
NATO	North American Treaty Organization
NAWC	National Association of Water Companies
NCS	National Communications System
NCUA	National Credit Union Administration
NEI	Nuclear Energy Institute

NERC	North American Electric Reliability Council
NFIB	National Federation of Independent Business
NGA	National Governors Association
NGC	Natural Gas Council
NGSA	National Gas Supply Association
NIST	National Institute of Standard and Technology
NPGA	National Propane Gas Association
NPRA	National Petroleum and Refiners Association
NRC	Nuclear Regulatory Commission
NRECA	National Rural Electric Cooperative Association
NRIC	Network Reliability and Interoperability Council
NSF	National Science Foundation
NSTAC	National Security Telecommunications Advisory Committee
OCC	Office of the Comptroller of the Currency
OECD	Organization for Economical Cooperation and Development
OIG	Office of the Inspector General
OMB	Office of Management Budget
OPM	Office of Personal Management
OTS	Office of Thrift Supervision
PBX	Private Branch Exchange Equipment
PCCIP	President's Commission on Critical Infrastructure Protection
PMAA	Petroleum Marketers Association of America
PN	Public Network
PSAP	Public Safety Answering Points
PSN	Public Switch Network
PTTC	Petroleum Technology Transfer Council
PUC	Public Utility Commission
PWBA	Pension and Welfare Benefits Administration
PWS	Public Water System
RUS	Rural Utilities Service
RTU	Remote Terminal Units

SBA	Small Business Administration
SCADA	Supervisory Control and Data Acquisition
SEC	Securities Exchange Commission
SIA	Securities Industry Association
USDA	United States Department of Agriculture
VA	Veterans Administration
WEMA	Water Equipment Manufacturers Association

Appendix III:
Y2K Solution Approaches

There are multiple solutions to the problem. Each has some merit, such as quick implementation time, and some drawbacks, such as limited ranges of applicability. For a relative comparison of these techniques and how long they take to implement, see figure 1.[1]

- *Data-date expansion:* Convert all two-digit dates to four digits in the data files.
- *Software-date expansion:* Handle the date expansion requirements in the software doing the calculation.
- *Compliant commercial software:* Purchase Y2K compliant software that meets your needs.
- *Binary date encoding:* Modify the software to represent dates at the bit level. Two bytes, or 16 bits, can account for over 65,000 years.
- *Database duplication:* Develop two- and four-digit versions of databases to work with compliant and non-compliant software.
- *Redevelop software:* Redo the application software so that it becomes compliant.

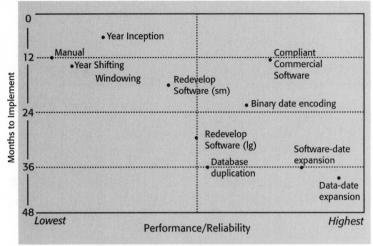

Figure 1: Relative Comparison of Y2K Solutions

- *Year interception:* Catch all date calculations and replace erroneous results with correct ones.
- *Windowing:* Choose an appropriate year, for example 1950, and process all years between 50 and 99 as 20th century dates, all years between 00 and 49 as 21st century dates.
- *Year shifting:* Use the 28-year cycle of the calendar and shift dates until all dates that need to be processed are in the same century.
- *Manual:* Reinstitute non-automated processes.

Notes

Foreword

1. Y2K is shorthand for Year 2000 (2 times k, which stands for kilo, which means 1000).
2. Gene Bylinsky, "Industry Wakes Up to the Year 2000 Problem," *Fortune*, 27 April 1998.
   (http://www.pathfinder.com/fortune/1998/980427.html)
3. Ibid.
4. Chapter 2 of *Connections*, on the rise of gold coins and trade, is also worth considering.
5. Transcripts of the papers presented at these hearings, though not questions and answers, are posted on the Committee's Web site:
   http://www.senate.gov/~Y2K/priorities.html.

Introduction

1. Y2K is an acronym that stands for the Year 2000. The letter K is scientific shorthand for 1000.
2. "Year 2000 Recession?," Edward Yardeni, Version 9.1, November 2, 1998, chapter 3, http://www.yardeni.com/Y2Kbook.html.
3. "Year 2000 Survival Guide," Edmund X. DeJesus, *BYTE Magazine*, July 1998, p. 57.

4. ITAA Press Release, March 25, 1998,
   http://www.itaa.org/Y2Kpr.htm.
5. "The Global Economic Impact of the Year 2000 Software Problem," Capers Jones, version 5.2, January 23, 1997, Software Productivity Research, Burlington, MA, pp. 57–58.
6. *Business Week,* December 14, 1998, p.39.
7. "The Global Economic Impact of the Year 2000 Software Problem," Capers Jones, version 5.2, January 23, 1997, Software Productivity Research, Burlington, MA, p. 20.
8. Critical Foundations: Protecting America's Critical Infrastructures (PCCIP report, October 1997).
9. Testimony of Sandia National Laboratories before the Special Committee on the Year 2000 Technology Problem, United States Senate, July 31, 1998.
10. Richard M. Nunno, "The Year 2000 Computer Problem: Activity in the 105th Congress," Congressional Research Service, October 1, 1998.

Utilities

1. The American Petroleum Institute (API), the Natural Gas Council (NGC), the American Gas Association (AGA), the American Public Gas Association (APGA), the Gas Research Institute (GRI), the Interstate Natural Gas Association of America (INGAA), the Independent Petroleum Association of America (IPAA), the Association of Oil Pipelines (AOPL), the Gas Processors Association (GPA), the National Gas Supply Association (NGSA), the Gas Industries Standards Board (GISB), the National Petroleum & Refiners Association (NPRA), the National Propane Gas Association (NPGA), the Petroleum Marketers Association of America (PMAA), and the Petroleum Technology Transfer Council (PTTC).
2. Congressional Research Service Briefing to Committee Staff on 06/02/98.

Telecommunications

1. *NRIC Network Interoperability: The Key to Competition,* July 15, 1997.
2. NCS report.

3. Testimony of Dr. Judith List, July 31, 1998.

4. The President's National Security Telecommunications Advisory Committee, *The Network Group Report on Y2K & Telecommunications,* September 10, 1998, page 2.

5. Year 2000—The Enemy within the Network (GSA Conference Presentation November 1998) Steve Prentice.

6. *NRIC Network Interoperability: The Key to Competition,* July 15, 1997.

7. *Assessment of the Year 2000 Impacts on the Public Network,* The National Communications System, October 1998.

8. Letter from Senator John Kyl (R-AZ) to FCC Chairman William Kennard, March 30, 1998.

9. Testimony of Gerard Roth before the Special Committee on the Year 2000 Technology Problem, July 31, 1998.

10. In April 1998, the Minnesota Department of Public Service surveyed 100 telephone utilities and received 84 responses. The results were encouraging: 75% had a Y2K project manager and 55% had developed detailed plans. Scott Reiter, National Telephone Cooperative Association, GSA Conference, October 21, 1998.

11. Ramu Potarazu, INTELSAT, Testimony before the Special Committee on the Year 2000 Technology Problem, July 31, 1998.

12. Ibid.

13. Louis Lavelle, "Programmers Racing to Head Off Computer Doomsday"; *The Bergen Record,* Bergen, New Jersey, Sunday, January 25, 1998. "Our customers have a lot to worry about," he said. "The thing about this whole year 2000 problem is we can get it right. But if everybody else doesn't get it all right, what is the point? We are only one link in the chain . . . we all have to get it right." (John Pasqua, AT&T)

14. The President's Commission Critical Infrastructure Protection, October 1997.

15. Ibid.

16. Ibid.

17. The JTRB membership includes senior staff from the FCC, NCS, Department of Defense, State, Commerce, Federal Emergency Management Agency, and General Services Agency.

18. Dr. Judith List, Bellcore.

19. Jack Grubman, "Financial Analysts See End to Market Turmoil," *Communications Daily,* October 7, 1998, pp. 7–8.

General Government

1. Public Law 93-288 was amended by Public Law 100-707 and retitled as the Robert T. Stafford Disaster Relief and Emergency Assistance Act (Public Law 93-288, as amended).

2. Under the Plan, a State means any State of the United States, the District of Columbia, Puerto Rico, Virgin Islands, Guam, American Samoa, Trust Territory of the Pacific Islands, Commonwealth of the Northern Mariana Islands, Federated States of Micronesia, or Republic of the Marshall Islands.

International Preparedness

1. OECD Report, The Year 2000 Problem: Impacts and Actions.

Appendix III

1. "Year 2000 Survival Guide," Edmund X. DeJesus, *BYTE Magazine*, July 1998, p. 53.

Also Available to Get You Prepared for Y2K

The Millennium Bug: How to Survive the Coming Chaos
By Michael S. Hyatt

In this *New York Times* best-seller, Michael S. Hyatt explains the impending Y2K catastrophe in simple terms and gives thirteen specific action steps to protect you and your family.

0-89526-334-3 • Hardcover • 228 pages
Also available on video: 0-7852-9447-3

Spiritual Survival During the Y2K Crisis
By Steve Farrar

Best-selling author Steve Farrar examines Y2K through the lens of biblical truth and helps you discover a practical plan for your family.

0-7852-7309-3 • Paperback • 252 pages

Y2K for Women: How to Protect Your Home and Family in the Coming Crisis
By Karen Anderson

In simple terms and without scare tactics, Karen Anderson gives specific advice to women on how to prepare for Y2K, where to find solutions you can trust, and what *not* to worry about.

0-7852-6853-7 • Paperback • 224 pages

The Y2K Personal Survival Guide
By Michael S. Hyatt

This one-stop, comprehensive book by best-selling author
Michael S. Hyatt explains the ins-and-outs of Y2K preparation—everything you need to know to get you and your family
from this side of the crisis to the other.

0-89526-301-7 • Hardcover • 360 pages

Y2K: The Day the World Shut Down
By Michael Hyatt and George Grant

A chilling novel about what could happen in the year 2000
when the world's computers shut down.

0-8499-1387-x • Paperback • 268 pages

Y2K: What Every Christian Should Know
By Michael S. Hyatt

In this special audio package, Michael S. Hyatt, author of the
New York Times best-seller *The Millennium Bug*, talks about
what the Millennium Bug is, how it will affect you, and what
Christians should do personally to prepare for the coming days.

0-7852-6933-9 • Audio • Two 90-minute cassettes